Adelaide Skeen

YOUR HOUSE IN NEEDLEPOINT

ALSO BY BARBARA L. FARLIE

BEADING: BASIC AND BOUTIQUE
PENNYWISE BOUTIQUE
ALL ABOUT DOLL HOUSES
    (with Charlotte L. Clarke)

YOUR
HOUSE
IN
NEEDLEPOINT

BARBARA L. FARLIE
and
CONSTANCE C. SLOAN

Needlepoint photographs by Otto Maya
Drawings by Jill Weber

Bobbs-Merrill
Indianapolis / New York

Published by The Bobbs-Merrill Company, Inc.
Indianapolis / New York

Designed by Helen Barrow
Manufactured in the United States of America
First paperbound printing, 1978

Library of Congress Cataloging in Publication Data

Farlie, Barbara L
  Your house in needlepoint.

  Includes index.
  1. *Canvas embroidery—Patterns.* I. Sloan,
Constance C., joint author.   II.   Title.
TT778.C3F37   746.4′4   75-511
ISBN 0-672-52055-9
ISBN 0-672-52056-7 Pbk.

To our families

for their interest, enthusiasm and help,
not only during the preparation of this book
but throughout our lives.

Contents

Four: BLOCKING AND FINISHING

YOUR HOUSE IN NEEDLEPOINT

Introduction

If there is one thing a family cherishes more than any other, it is their home. We all take great pride in our homes—we carefully furnish and decorate them and, as time passes, look back on them with great fondness. Our homes represent our personalities, and remind us of cherished times spent with loved ones. There are very few ways of preserving these memories that don't require a great deal of creative effort, ability or expense. If you are an artist, you can do a pen-and-ink sketch, a watercolor or an oil painting of your home, but the vast majority of us must content ourselves with snapshots and home movies.

Re-creating your house in needlepoint is a new approach to a centuries-old art. Here you are both designer and artist, and your finished canvas will reflect in a wholly personal way all the aspects of your home that mean most to you.

What makes the finished product so unusual and such a departure from conventional needlepoint is the use of varying stitches to reproduce the textures of wood, brick, stone, even the shrubs in your garden. Each portrait is a delightful combination of stitches from needle arts such as bargello, crewel and other embroidery, all adapted to working on canvas.

The possibilities for textural expression with this method are practically endless. Even in a house that is all the same color, its various components will stand out clearly in their different textures. Your finished picture will have a three-dimensional quality, giving it a most lifelike appearance—you will almost be able to anticipate the front door opening and someone stepping out to greet you.

In addition, our method is such fun and works up so quickly that you will enjoy watching it come to life before your eyes. We can almost guarantee that you'll complete your needlepoint house in record time. And because the procedure is so simple, you will need only a few pieces of basic and inexpensive equipment.

If you can't draw or paint, don't worry. As you will soon see, with the help of a snapshot and a ruler, a sharp pencil and charting paper, you can easily begin to create your portrait without any special artistic ability. In fact, those of you without experience in needlepoint may even have a slight edge over the needlework pro, because you won't be locked into traditional methods.

We give you complete instructions from the beginning, from your first outline of the house, transferring your design onto canvas and stitching it, right through to the final blocking and framing or otherwise finishing of the completed portrait. We present over forty stitches (for windows, doors, roofs, facades, landscapes and backgrounds), showing you how to choose those that best portray your house and how to work them— with complete how-to diagrams and detail work-ups in full color guiding you every step of the way.

And in Part Three you will see a wide selection of completed portraits in many styles from traditional through modern—each shown in full color, with an analysis of its composition and a discussion of its design problems and their solutions. We selected them because they are generally representative of houses found everywhere today, and you will doubtless find many aspects and features of your own house among them. Thus, as you look through, you will gather many ideas for stitches and effects as well as design solutions useful for any house you plan to portray in needlepoint.

The picture you create will be particularly handsome when framed and hung on a wall where it can be admired, but there are many other ways to show it off. Imagine it covering a piano bench or a footstool, or as a pillow. You can frame it under glass, add handles and use it as a serving tray, both decorative and functional. The same tray would be especially handsome set on small legs to serve as a coffee table. Or you can even carry it around with you, appliqued onto a tote bag—the possibilities are endless.

In these times of increasing mobility, with families moving all over the country every few years, it is a wonderful way to preserve your memories of places you have lived in. All you need is a snapshot to start with—of a vacation cottage, even of your childhood home or a well-known landmark in your town. (The schoolhouse portrayed in Chapter 13 is an example of the latter.) You may also want to create someone else's house in needlepoint as a very special birthday, Christmas or anniversary present for people you love.

Whatever house you portray, you will have the added pleasure of creating a family heirloom—to be passed on to future generations to cherish as we do the embroidered samplers passed on to us from earlier times. Best of all, you will have the incomparable satisfaction of knowing that yours is a one-of-a-kind creation, and that you made it yourself, from start to finish.

We would like to express our deep appreciation to the following people for allowing us to share with you the needlepoint portraits of their homes: Mr. and Mrs. William N. Farlie, Mr. and Mrs. Mortimer J. Fox, Jr., Mrs. Joseph F. Hanlon, Mr. and Mrs. Herman W. Leitzow, Mr. and Mrs. Edward F. Serban, Mr. and Mrs. Frederick C. Smith. We also owe a debt of gratitude to Vivian M. Abell, Natalie Bellet, Pat Longley, and to a number of students in the Montclair Adult School in Montclair, New Jersey.

Barbara L. Farlie
Constance C. Sloan

One
THE
FIRST STEPS

1. Supplies and Tools

Fortunately, you need very little equipment to portray your house in needlepoint. Furthermore, many of the required supplies and tools are kept on hand in most households, so you will not have to invest a lot of money in new or fancy materials.

CANVAS

There are two kinds of needlepoint canvas, mono and penelope, which come in a variety of sizes. Mono canvas is made up of single threads woven together to form the mesh; in other words, mono canvas is woven much like a loosely woven fabric. Mono canvas is recommended for needlepoint portraits, chiefly because the more dense double-woven penelope canvas is difficult to draw or calculate on without making mistakes.

The best mono canvas for your picture is called Interlock, or Locked Weave; instead of the threads crossing over and under each other as in plain mono canvas, the threads in the Interlock mono cross *through* each other, locking the meshes together. As it is less thick than other canvases, Interlock mono is easier to paint on and see through—important for creating a needlepoint picture. It also holds stitches

in place securely and does not tend to twist out of shape while being worked on.

For best visibility and ease of stitching, buy white mono canvas, preferably Interlock, in sizes 13 or 14, which have respectively 13 or 14 meshes to the inch. (Or use size 6 in the metric system, with 6 meshes to the centimeter.) You can include a lot of detail on size 13 or 14 Interlock mono canvas and still have a picture of appropriate size, whereas a size 12 canvas (only 12 meshes to the inch) would work out to a larger picture than most people want.

Available in needlework shops and in some craft shops, canvas is sold by the yard (90 cm.) with a width of approximately 40 inches (1 meter). It can be used in the length or the width, depending on whether you have a tall or a wide house to portray. All of the houses shown in this book were done on half a yard of canvas or less. So, unless your house is unusually large, it is safe to buy half a yard of canvas and trim later as needed.

YARN

The best yarn for a needlepoint house project is Persian, found in needlework and large craft shops and in department stores. Persian yarn can be purchased by the ounce, but for most needlepoint house projects, which may have small spots of various colors, it is better to buy single strands of yarn. A strand of Persian yarn is about 1 yard (90 cm.) long and consists of three two-ply threads that are twisted together but can be separated easily. Most of the stitches on a size 13 or 14 Interlock mono canvas will be executed with two of the three threads in a strand of yarn. Separate two of the three threads and use them, then later combine the remaining single thread with the remaining single thread from the next strand you pull out; essentially, you obtain 3 yards of thread from every 2 yards (270 cm. from every 180 cm.) of Persian yarn. You can also buy yarn by the packet or skein.

Persian yarn is recommended because it works up nicely in rather small meshes of canvas and it comes in a wide range of beautiful colors. A possible substitute for Persian yarn is the Persian-type yarn often used for crewel work, but the color choice is not nearly as wide. Do not use left-over knitting yarn for needlepoint, as it will not cover the canvas nor wear as well.

In addition to Persian yarn, you may also need several colors of silk buttonhole twist, carpet thread, and even embroidery floss for detail work that will be embroidered or placed over pre-worked areas. If you don't already have them on hand, these items can be purchased at a fabric or sewing shop when the need arises.

NEEDLES

#18 or #20 tapestry needles are required to stitch a needlepoint picture. These are the blunt-ended needles with large eyes; they are available wherever you buy your yarn. You may also need a few embroidery needles for embroidery or overlay work.

MARKING TOOLS AND SUPPLIES

You will need a few sharp #2 lead pencils, a sharp-edged eraser, and a clear plastic ruler for charting your house design onto a photocopy of your canvas as described in chapter 4). You will also need a sheet of gray construction paper. For transfering the design onto the canvas you will need a set of primary color acrylic paints and a few small, fine-tipped, nylon artist's brushes; these can be bought in art supply stores and craft and hobby shops, and are inexpensive. Acrylic paint in tubes requires the addition of water before painting; acrylic paint in jars can be used as is. The brushes clean up easily when washed in water.

The advantages of acrylic paint are that it dries quickly and is waterproof, the latter being extremely important in the event your canvas needs dampening during the blocking process.

You may put your design onto the canvas with permanent color markers instead of acrylic paints, as long as the markers are clearly labeled "waterproof" or "permanent color." (Even then, be sure to test them to make sure they won't bleed, even slightly, when dampened.) As with acrylics, the markers are widely available, inexpensive, and can be purchased in sets. Fine-tipped markers are preferable for detail work, wide-tipped for large areas of color. If you like, you can use both acrylics and markers on a single project, employing markers for the bare outlines and the acrylics for filling in.

OTHER TOOLS AND SUPPLIES

You will need masking tape to bind the raw edges of your canvas after you have cut it to size, to keep the edges from ravelling as you work. Though ravelling is less likely with the Interlock mono canvas, masking tape is still recommended because it adds firmness to the edges, and the yarn will not catch on them as you are stitching. One inch (2.5 cm.), or slightly narrower, masking tape is fine, or you can trim wider masking tape to size if you have some on hand.

You will also need a pair of small, sharp, pointed scissors—either embroidery or mani-cure—to trim off yarn at the end of stitching, and some rust-proof straight pins or tacks for blocking the completed canvas. You may need some staples and a stapler for attaching the blocked canvas to the backing preparatory to framing.

But first of all you are going to need a camera and some film to take a snapshot of the house you intend to portray in needlepoint, as we explain in the next chapter.

2. Your House and Its Features

The first step toward portraying your house in needlepoint is to take a snapshot of it. This will help you decide on the view and details you wish to include. (It will also be used later for scaling-up and charting, as described in Chapter 4.) A clear 3 x 4″ (7.5 x 10 cm.) snapshot in color or black and white is suitable. It can be taken at any time of day as long as the view of the house is clear. Thus, if dense foliage blocks most of your view, you should take the photograph in winter or early spring.

The front of a house is usually the best view and should be photographed directly head on. However, if you cannot place yourself precisely in front, you may stand slightly to the side, or lower or higher—but later, when charting the house, you will have to readjust it to eliminate sections that would not be visible head on, or add sections that would.

Though generally not as interesting as the front, the back view may sometimes be preferable, especially when it features beautiful landscaping, a terrace or a pool. The back view of the Norman French house in Chapter 16 was considered the most desirable to portray in needlepoint.

A side or a three-quarter view of a house are other alternatives. But the three-quarter view will definitely present problems with perspective, since the view requires angles and slanted lines, both difficult to achieve on the straight horizontal and vertical lines of your canvas. Still, the three-quarter view can be used if the perspective is handled by making window-panes on the canvas smaller and smaller as they recede; you will see how these problems are handled in the three-quarter portrait of the Town Schoolhouse in Chapter 13.

Try to include in your photograph what you want to put into your needlepoint picture—namely, the house and a few contiguous trees and shrubs. Omit the garage, unless attached to the house, and if possible, the driveway. Don't be concerned if the photograph does not reproduce minute details, such as the lines of wood siding or coach lights beside the front door; that is not the purpose of the photograph.

As you undoubtedly know, a photograph will exaggerate any important feature out in front, like a stone wall, picket fence, or iron gates like those in front of the Georgian Colonial house in Chapter 12. Naturally, you have to scale them down a bit for your portrait, for otherwise they would loom up enormously in proportion to the house—hardly the effect you want to achieve.

Your needlepoint portrayal will be *almost* lifelike, but not quite. Certain features of a house will tend to look flat—porches, cornices and roof overhangs are prime examples—though there are certain "fool the eye" techniques for showing depth, which we discuss in

Chapters 4, 6 and 7. Still, you must keep in mind that your needlepoint picture is a representation, not a reproduction.

We should mention that if you possess considerable talent for drafting, you can work from a simple sketch of your house instead of from a photograph. However, a drawing is never as accurate as a clear photograph. Take a look at the two treatments of a Dutch Colonial house in Chapter 10. The first treatment—white house and red door—was done from a drawing; the second—yellow house and dark green door—was done from a photograph. At first glance the white house seems to have correct proportions, but when you compare it to the photograph and to the yellow house, you can see it is less than accurate. In addition, the white house has a simple, almost primitive quality, which again is the result of using a drawing as a guide. But we don't want to imply that the primitive look is less attractive; it is simply a matter of the style you prefer.

YOUR HOUSE IN A NEW LIGHT

As you study your photograph, we recommend you step outside your house and spend ample time studying it and its surroundings. The more you examine it, the more aware you will become of its details. Eventually, as you memorize the features, especially the more unusual ones, you will be able to determine which of them to include in your picture and which to minimize or leave out altogether. Begin, of course, with the more obvious features: the number of windows, number of chimneys, materials of the facade and roof, door treatment, porches, foliage, and so forth. With these in mind, you can proceed to note the details. For example, if the facade is brick, is the brick set evenly, randomly, or in a herringbone pattern? How many panes are in each window, and which windows, if any, have shutters? If the

siding is clapboard, are the boards wide or narrow?

When you have concluded a thorough examination, you can begin to decide which details are important to your representation. Those that are especially handsome and noteworthy—such as a beautiful doorway, columns, unusual stone work—should be included even though they are frequently difficult to portray. Other details—such as an immense ivy or wisteria vine—tend to dominate a house and so you should try merely to suggest them instead of capturing their full scope. You may take other liberties with foliage, too—especially with shrubbery—by making its shape more ideal, lowering or heightening it, filling in where it is sparse in reality.

THE FIRST ROUGH SKETCH

Once you have thought through all the details, you are ready to draw a preliminary rough sketch of the over-all design. Using your photograph as a guide, as well as your study of the actual house, take a piece of scratch paper and draw a rough sketch of the house as you want to portray it; Diagram 1 below is a sample of

Diagram 1

such a sketch. The size is irrelevant; what you are striving for is a better grasp of your design before you choose stitches or chart it. Try to get on paper a feeling of the house and its surroundings. Decide absolutely what you want to include, and exercise artistic license where appropriate. For example, if there is a lovely old oak tree on your property but it is just out of sight in the photograph, pull the tree into the sketch, placing it closer to the house than it really is. If it gives you the desired effect, you should definitely keep it in the picture.

Problems of perspective should be resolved in this sketch, too. The base lines of any object that you want to appear forward in the picture should be drawn lower than the base lines of other objects. Steps should appear to come toward you by making each advancing step a little wider or a little deeper. Sidewalks and driveways should be angled out.

And, incidentally, if you are planning to repaint the outside of the house in the near future in a different color or colors, be sure to use the new colors in your needlepoint picture, so the representation will be accurate for a number of years.

Mansard slate   Tile   Wood shingle   Slate

ROOFS

Arborvitae-type   Yew-type   Hemlock-type   Rhododendron-type

SHRUBS

TREES

Palm   Birch   Fir

wear. On the other hand, the make-believe house of Chapter 4 would make a great pillow, because the work is very tight, in spite of a bit of embroidery work. In general, if you have any doubts about the durability of certain stitches in your picture, we recommend that you put it on a wall or under a piece of glass, say as a small table top or a tray.

Once you have determined the size and purpose of your needlepoint portrait, you can buy your piece of canvas, making sure to get slightly more than you need so that while you are stitching the canvas, there is an unworked border of at least an inch (2.5 cm.) all the way around.

A last piece of advice: after you have made a tentative decision as to your stitches, we strongly recommend that you experiment with all of them on some scraps of canvas, for it is only when you see a stitch worked up that you can be certain of its effectiveness for the purpose you have in mind.

4. Charting your Design

Charting is the process of getting your house design onto paper, in the same size it will be on your canvas.

The first step is to make a photocopy of the half-yard of canvas you've bought—the photocopy will be a duplicate of the canvas meshes; thus any design you draw on it will be the exact size for your stitching. (Note: don't try to use graph paper as a substitute for the photocopy: graph paper grids won't correspond to your canvas grids, and this would throw off all your charting.)

You'll need the following supplies: transparent adhesive tape, scissors, sharp pencils, an eraser, a clear plastic ruler, and a piece of gray construction paper (which comes in sheets somewhat larger than legal size, and is available in stationery stores). The construction paper is placed over your canvas on the photocopy machine to make a background—it's essential to use medium gray to provide the proper contrast against the white canvas meshes.

THE PHOTOCOPY

Locate a nearby photocopy machine—you'll probably find one in your local library, bank or post office, as well as in commercial printing establishments or office supply stores. Copies generally cost about ten cents each. Since your canvas will probably be too large to fit on the machine, you'll have to make several smaller copies and piece them together to proper size. (You should also make a few spare copies for charting practice.)

When you're ready to start photocopying, read the directions on the machine, and set it to make a legal-size copy. Then place the *short* side of your canvas straight against the *long* side of the copying area, as shown in diagram 2—be sure to line it up accurately, as shown. Next, place the gray construction paper over the canvas on the copier, as indicated by the broken line in diagram 2. Set the machine for the number of copies you want, and press the print button.

MAKING YOUR CHARTING PAPER

Take your photocopies home, and lay out on a table as many of them as you need to duplicate the size of your canvas. For most projects, two or three copies placed side by side (as in diagram 3) will be large enough, as you need only enough to accommodate the design area. With scissors, trim the long sides of your copies about ¼" (6 mm.) along a white thread line. Then overlap the copies, *long sides together*, about ¼"—make sure the white threads are lined up perfectly. Carefully tape them together

Diagram 2

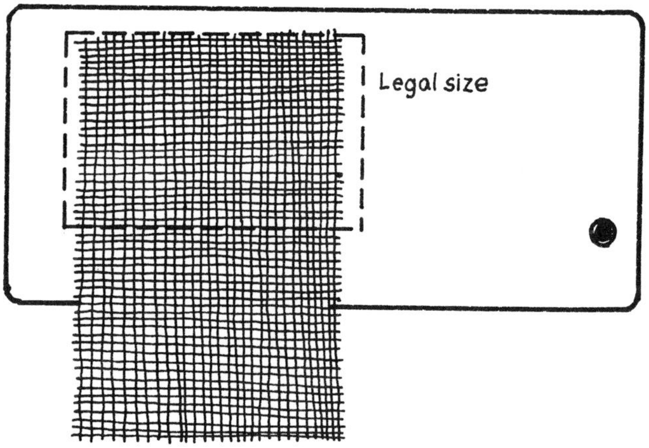

Legal size

Diagram 3

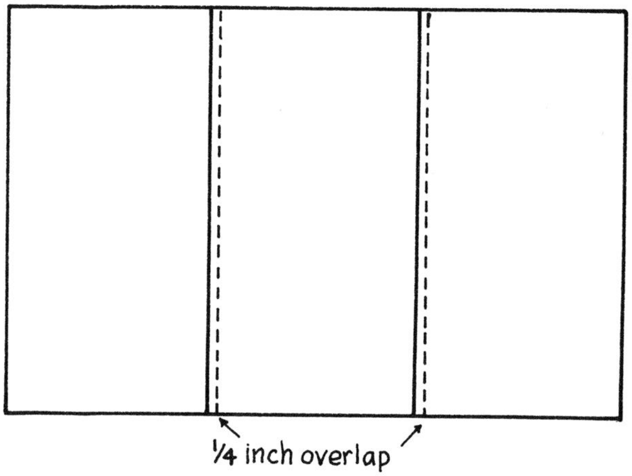

¼ inch overlap

Diagram 4

on the front, using transparent adhesive tape on which you can write.

You now have a full size copy of your canvas. This is your charting paper, which is how we refer to it from now on.

SCALING-UP THE MAKE-BELIEVE HOUSE

Next you draw your house design onto the charting paper—scaling it up to proper size from your original small snapshot. To show you how to do it, we are using a small make-believe house and charting all its features, so you can learn the principles before charting your own. The only difference is that we'll be using a small drawing (diagram 4) instead of a real snapshot.

Our purpose is to establish the final size of our canvas design in relation to the size of our small drawing (diagram 4). That is, how much larger will the canvas design be—twice as large? larger? Once we establish this for an important feature, the rest of the house will naturally scale-up in the same proportion. To do this, we choose our stitches for that feature, and measure their size when worked up.

In our make-believe house, we start with the multi-paned windows, as they dominate the look of the facade. We chose Cashmere stitch (Code: D-1) for the panes, Continental stitch (Code: B-2) for the window frame, and Reverse Alternating Tent stitch (Code: D-9) for the shutters—these are the stitches that most accurately portray them. (You will find all these stitches, as coded, complete with working diagrams, in chapter 6.)

FINDING THE SIZE OF
THE FINISHED WINDOW

First we work out the width: looking at the stitch diagram, we see that Cashmere stitch takes 2 canvas threads across for each pane;

there are four panes across, making a total of 8 canvas threads for the panes. Continental stitch takes 1 canvas thread for the frame on each side, for a total of 2. Reverse Alternating tent stitch takes 3 canvas threads for each shutter, for a total of 6. Thus we know the completed window plus shutters will be 16 threads wide.

We work out the height in the same way: Cashmere stitch takes 3 canvas threads down for each pane; there are four panes down, making a total of 12 canvas threads. Continental stitch takes 1 canvas thread for the frame, top and bottom, for a total of 2—making the entire window 14 threads high.

We now know the completed window will be 16 canvas threads wide and 14 threads high.

THE FIRST CHARTING

Now we take a spare piece of charting paper and draw the outlines of the completed window. We count out 16 threads in width and 14 in height and draw a pencil line around them (diagram 5). Note that we always draw pencil outlines between canvas threads—thus we easily see the number of threads within any particular feature, stitch or color. (And later, when we align the canvas over the charting paper, the design will be clearly visible, as it's drawn between the threads, not on them.)

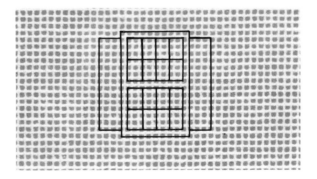

Diagram 5

ESTABLISHING THE SCALE

We measure the width of the window on our small drawing (diagram 4)—as you see, it's a little more than ½" (13 mm.) wide. Then we measure it as charted—and it is about twice the size of the drawing. This means that everything else will have to be about twice as large to be in the same scale. So we have established a 2-to-1 scale for charting our make-believe house.

Until now, we've been counting out, thread by thread, to establish the width of that window. From now on, we'll work to the established scale, making our outlines twice as large as they are in our small drawing (diagram 4), and adjusting if stitches require it. (Though it might seem logical to use a photostat of the small drawing enlarged to proper size, this won't work just because the stitches don't always come out to exact ratio, and must be adjusted.)

TESTING THE SCALE

Before charting all of our make-believe house, we'll test the 2-to-1 scale on another major feature—the door—to make sure it really works out. We test by measuring the door on our small drawing (diagram 4)—just the door, not the columns around it. It measures almost ⅜ x ¾" (9 x 18 mm.). Multiplying by 2, we see that our charted door should be about ¾ x 1½" (18 x 36 mm.).

On our spare piece of charting paper we mark these outlines for the door and count the threads within them: 10 threads across and 20 in height. Now we'll see if our stitches fit, and we find they do, perfectly, as shown in diagram 6.

Testing the width: For the two square top door panels, we chose the square Scotch stitch (Code: D-7) which takes 3 canvas threads across, for a total of 6 threads across. (For

Diagram 6

the lower panels, the same width, we used the Cashmere stitch (Code: D-1), which gives the same surface look, though the panels are higher.) For the remainder of the door frame, we used Continental stitch (Code: B-2), using 2 threads between the panels and 1 on each side—thus the door will total 10 threads across.

Testing the height: the fanlight, very tiny in the small drawing (diagram 4), we made 3 threads high and set it 2 threads below the top. (It is worked in the same Continental stitch as the surrounding frame, but in a different color, with overlay embroidery (Code: E-3) marking the divisions.) With 1 row of Continental stitch below the fanlight, this takes 6 threads. The top panels, 3 threads high with 1 row of Continental stitch below them, take another 4. We used 9 threads for the lower panels and 1 for the bottom door frame—a total of 20 canvas threads in height.

Thus we know the scale really works out, and from now on the going is easy—we'll measure all outlines and details of our drawing (diagram 4) and double those measurements on our charting paper.

CHARTING THE MAKE-BELIEVE HOUSE

Placement is simple: looking at diagram 4, we see there are trees on both sides, with the house roughly centered between them. So the house will be roughly centered on the charting paper. *Roughly* is the word: measure any part of diagram 4 and compare it with the charting paper (diagram 7) and you'll find slight variations—windows placed up or down a thread; the outside lines moved out or in a bit, depending how they look in proportion to everything else.

CHARTING THE OUTLINES AND HOUSE DETAILS

In principle, we establish the house outlines first, then chart the roof and the important features of the facade. You can follow us on diagram 7, as we go. We measured the width and height of the house in diagram 4, multiplied by two and drew in the house outline shown in diagram 7. We set the top roof line just inside the house walls, and the lower roof line just outside them. To show the top trim line of the facade, we allowed 1 row of Continental stitch (Code: B-2) just under the lower roof line.

Now we had the bare outlines of our house with nothing inside. We began adding details, starting with the door we had already charted (diagram 6). We set it correctly below the roof line (twice the distance shown in diagram 4), then outlined it (20 x 10 threads), well centered, with space for the steps below it.

For the porch columns we chose the Tramé Straight Gobelin stitch (Code: D-10). Diagram 4 shows the columns slightly to the side of the door, so we left 1 thread between them (to be done in the same stitch as the house facade).

The columns are 2 threads higher than the door, and we set the porch roof on them, curving the underside to approximate the curve in diagram 4. For the porch roof we chose Continental stitch (Code: B-2), with edges emphasized by Split stitch (Code: D-8).

We charted the door sill (1 row of Continental stitch (Code: B-2), and the steps below (Straight Gobelin stitch (Code: D-3), allowing 2 threads per step. Note that the slightly wider bottom step helps give perspective.

Next we took our windows (16 x 14 threads each) as previously charted in diagram 5, centering them on either side of the door, placing upper and lower storeys in correct relation to each other and to the roof line.

An approximation is all we tried for—while we constantly measured diagram 4 as a check, a true scale-up of all the small parts isn't possible or even necessary. Once your outlines and central details are in place, your eye is the best guide—and that's what makes the charting so much fun.

For the flower boxes on the lower windows, we used Straight Gobelin stitch (Code: D-3) with Slanted Gobelin stitch (Code: D-2) at the sides. (Note that they cover the lower window frame.) We don't chart the flowers, as they are done after stitching is complete, using the various overlay embroidery stitches (Code: E-1 to 5) as we like. The color photographs of the two finished needlepoint versions on pages 38-39 show how we worked them.

The remaining house detail is the second storey window above the front door. It's about as wide as the other windows with shutters, so we allowed it the same 16 threads of width. The panes are smaller, so we used Mosaic stitch (Code: D-6), which is 2 threads square.

We used Continental stitch (Code: B-2) for the frame, centering it over the door below it.

Now we positioned the chimney (measuring, or placing it by eye). We used Brick stitch (Code: H-3), 6 threads high and wide. The top edge is Continental stitch (Code: B-2), extending out on either side.

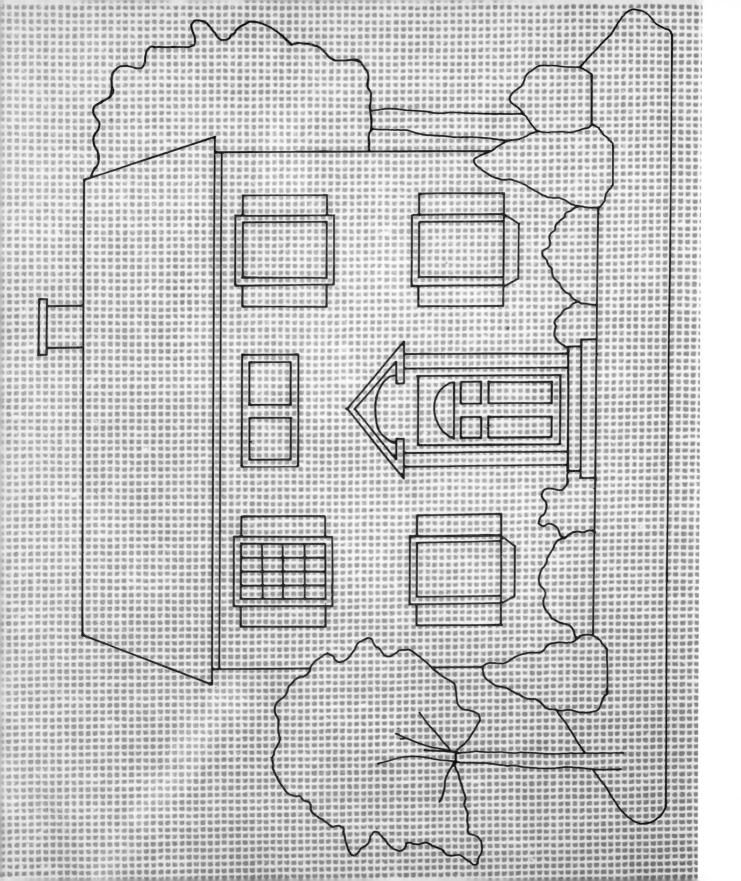

CHARTING THE SHRUBBERY, TREES AND GATE POSTS

The baseline of the shrubs is generally the same as the house foundation line. As we see in diagram 4, the evergreens at the corners are a bit forward of the shrubs—and we showed this by placing their baselines 2 threads lower. The shrub at far right is behind, on the side, and we placed its baseline 1 thread higher than the other shrubs, thus giving it a natural perspective. We charted the tops of the shrubs very casually, without concern for artistry—we made them tall and tapered, round and full, lower and higher—any way that gives the right effect. (And we erased any house lines falling within them.)

The tree at left is in front, and we placed it by eye, a few threads lower than the corner evergreen to give it proper perspective. We measured it on diagram 4, then charted it very generally to shape. Then we did the same for the tree on the right, placing it behind the shrubs and half-hidden by the house.

Finally we charted the brick gate posts (measuring, or placing them by eye). We set them a little below the base of the shrubs, and a little wider apart than the width of the bottom step. Like the chimney, they'll be worked in Brick stitch (Code: H-3), with the top row in Continental stitch (Code: B-2).

To give the walk its perspective, we angled it out from the steps down to the inner edge of the gate posts. (We didn't draw in the fencing, as that, too, will be done in overlay embroidery (Code: E-3) after all stitching is done—see it on the color photographs.)

We completed our charting by drawing in the lower grass lines—angling them up and in, to give a nice perspective.

When the design was complete, we darkened all the charted lines with a soft dark pencil (or indelible felt-tip marker) for good visibility—and it was ready to be transferred to canvas, and stitched.

Though it's only a make-believe house, we thought you'd like to see how it evolved from our drawing (diagram 4) to the chart (diagram 7) to a finished needlepoint portrait. Actually we did it in two versions—in red brick and in yellow clapboard—to show how different the same house looks with different colors and textures. You'll find them both on pages 38-39.

HELPFUL REMINDERS FOR CHARTING YOUR OWN HOUSE

1. Follow your snapshot carefully—checking the relationship of one area to another as you chart.

2. Mark pencil lines *between* white lines on photocopy.

3. Mark lightly until the design is complete.

4. Darken design lines before transferring to canvas.

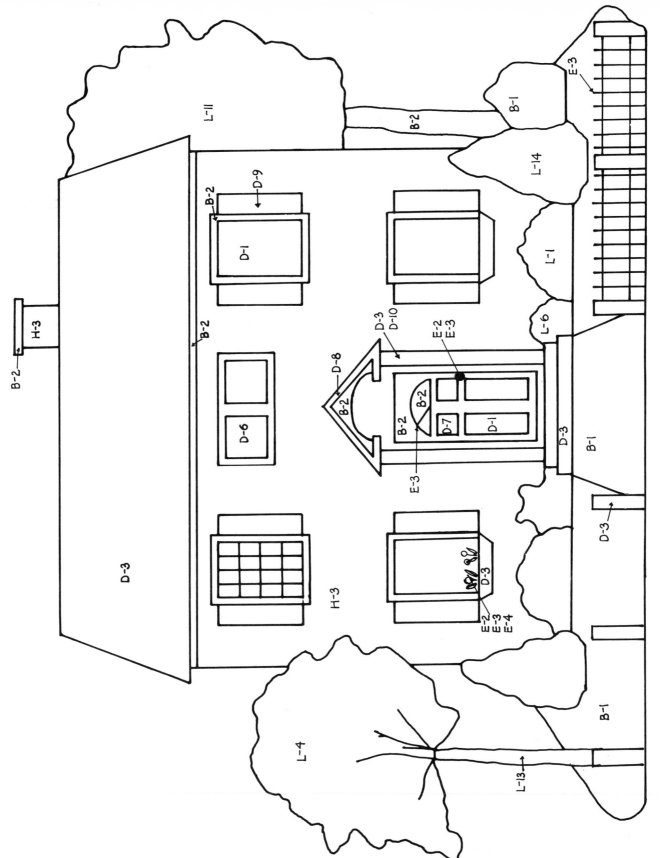

Stitching chart for red brick version of make-believe house

Stitching chart for yellow clapboard version of make-believe house

MAKE-BELIEVE HOUSE (red brick version)

MAKE-BELIEVE HOUSE (yellow clapboard version)

5. Transferring the Design to Canvas

Essentially there are three ways to transfer a charted design to your canvas. One is to use a gray permanent marker for the outlines only; the second is to paint on the design in all its colors, using acrylic paints. The third is a combination of these two: outlining in gray, and then painting colors within the outlines. Each has its advantages and we'll discuss them below, but whatever your method, there are a few preparations to start with.

The first is to attach your charting paper with the completed design onto a flat, uncluttered surface. The best thing for this is masking tape, which goes on and off easily and leaves no sticky residue. The best surface is of glass—a glass-top patio table or a piece of glass suspended between two tables of the same height. You can also tape the charting paper to a window, but only if you're using the first method of transferring. The advantage of a glass surface is that you can put a light underneath, which will make the lines of the charting paper extremely clear (though it does tend to blur the lines of the canvas). If you have no glass surface, a kitchen or a card table will do just as well, *if* you have a strong, unobstructed light overhead.

You should bind the raw edges of your canvas with masking tape 1″ (2.5 cm.) wide or slightly narrower. Place the tape on the canvas edge with half the width overhanging it. Cut the tape to the correct length, and fold it over the canvas edge to bind. Repeat for the other raw edges.

Place the canvas directly on top of the charting paper, allowing for a little margin at the bottom or top if you intend to stitch in your name, initials or some other wording there. Make absolutely certain the canvas threads line up perfectly with the white lines representing the threads on the charting paper. For instance, if the tops of windows are in line on the chart, the same horizontal canvas thread should line up with the tops of all those windows.

If the canvas is out of shape in any spot so you have difficulty lining it up, press it with a steam iron. (Or you can line it up as best you can over the important design areas and compensate later for where it is "off," but this is a nuisance and can lead to trouble.)

When everything is perfectly aligned, tape the canvas to the work surface along the top and down the side edges a short distance from the top. Leave the lower sides and the bottom loose, so you can lift up the canvas and look under it when transferring, if necessary.

THE THREE TRANSFER METHODS

MARKING OUTLINES ONLY
With this method you use a gray, permanent color marker with a fine tip to color the first

Diagram 8

canvas threads on the outer edges of a total area, such as a window or a door. Illustration 8 shows how the lines drawn on these threads indicate only the exterior house, roof and feature lines, and the areas encompassing the glass panes of the windows and the shutters. You don't need to indicate the window frames—you know where they begin and end, because you can see them on your charting paper. (Diagram 8.)

Place your gray lines carefully, and don't make them too dark or they may remain visible under certain light-colored yarns. With this method, the lines are only a guide, so draw the ones you think you need most and forget about details. If you make a mistake with the gray marker, correct it with white acrylic paint.

PAINTING ON THE DESIGN

Here you paint the entire design directly onto the canvas with acrylic paints. As illustration 9 shows, each complete area is painted a color to match the yarn that will cover it. Although the paint doesn't have to match the yarn exactly, these acrylics can be mixed to create virtually any desired color.

For this method we suggest you make a handy paint palette by covering a dinner plate with aluminum foil. You will also need two nylon-tipped artist's paint brushes, one very tiny and the other a bit larger, a paper cup filled with water, and some paper towels for absorbing excess water and cleaning off the brushes.

Place dabs of paint around the edges of the palette, taking care not to squeeze out too much paint if you are using tubes, because a little paint goes a long way. Use the center of the palette for mixing colors. Thin the paints with a little water on your brush to a consistency slightly thicker than water color paint. A tiny dot of paint when thinned with water will cover a large area of canvas, so don't mix more than you need at any one time. Another reason

Diagram 9

for mixing small amounts is that acrylics dry very quickly when exposed to air.

Apply paint to the canvas sparingly. If you accidentally load up the brush with paint, blot away the excess with a clean paper towel. When you apply paint sparingly, you'll also find it much easier to paint out any mistakes with white acrylic paint. If you discover a mistake after you've done the surrounding areas, you can correct it when stitching, by moving across, up or down the number of threads you are "off."

Because correct placement of windows and doors is essential, we recommend you paint them on your canvas first, then work out gradually to the larger areas. If the facade of your house happens to be gray, paint the windows a lighter gray so you can distinguish between them. Continue with any other gray areas, such as steps, sidewalk and perhaps the roof.

After painting all the features of the house, you can paint in the landscaping. Do not paint trees and shrubs any larger than they will be when stitched. In fact, it's wise to paint them slightly smaller, because you can easily enlarge them when stitching, whereas if you paint them too large, the green underpainting may show through a pale background.

You don't have to paint areas that are going to be white. If some definition is needed within a large area of white or at its edges, use a pale gray paint or marking pen.

MARKING OUTLINES AND PAINTING ON THE DESIGN

The third method is a combination of the other two. First you outline the house, its chief details and surroundings with the pale gray marking pen, then you paint everything with acrylics in their designated colors.

WHICH METHOD IS BEST FOR YOU?

There are advantages and disadvantages to each transfer method. Obviously, marking the outlines is easiest and quickest and tends to be favored by people who have never painted on canvas. The drawback is that specks of canvas may show through the stitches after you've worked them, especially the looser stitches. However, you can solve this problem by touching up any visible canvas with appropriate colored markers. For this we recommend using water color markers instead of indelible color, because the former come in a much wider color range. If only tiny spots of canvas show through, you can touch up before blocking without being concerned about the colors bleeding. If you have a lot of bare canvas spots, wait to color them until after the canvas is blocked, to avoid any bleeding of the ink.

The second method, painting on the design, gives you a canvas that is more attractive and more enjoyable to stitch; you will even find that it's a conversation piece among friends. Furthermore, this method leaves no question in your mind about where color details begin and end. And wherever the yarn doesn't completely cover the canvas, the paint behind the yarn will act as camouflage for the gaps.

But there are disadvantages. It takes more time to paint the canvas than to draw outlines with a marker, and the painted canvas takes longer to dry. If you don't intend to stitch in the background, you must be very careful not to let paint spill onto this area, as well as to exercise caution at the edges of the house and roof. In fact, if you have small children, you should do your painting while they're napping or in school to avoid any accidental jostling.

The third method, combining outline and paint, is probably the most comfortable for people with average needlepoint skills. Not only does it provide an attractive canvas to work on, it involves the least labor or concern when stitching. Here the paint acts as your color guide, while the outlines provide maximum control over where you begin and end a stitch.

Visibility will be the biggest problem with any of these methods. Whenever a line or detail on your charting paper is unclear, don't hesitate to look under the canvas, which will not shift since it is taped to the work surface.

With all of these methods, we recommend you note the position of a new area in relation to one already outlined or painted before starting on the new area. This is particularly relevant when you've calculated for a specific number of threads to execute a detail. For instance, if a window pane requires four threads and you suddenly discover there are only three threads left, simply move up or down a thread to compensate for the error. Of course this means you'll be marking a thread in an adjacent area, but this is acceptable so long as you keep it in mind later, when stitching.

In conclusion, do not fret about the transfer process. Many learners find this stage the most pleasurable—it has even inspired some of them to attempt further artistic projects they would not have dreamed of doing otherwise. And do remember that unless your background is to remain unfinished, the entire canvas will eventually be covered with yarn, which will also cover up any little mistakes.

Two
THE STITCHES
AND THE STITCHING

6. How to Work the Needlepoint Stitches

Although there are several hundred needle-point stitches, we have included only those that are most effective in recreating a realistic house and landscape. They are also the easiest and quickest to work up.

THE STITCH CODES

The stitches are organized by category according to the area of your picture where they would most likely be used, and coded as follows: Architectural detail stitches: Code D; House stitches: Code H; Landscape stitches: Code L; Embroidery and overlay stitches: Code E; Basic background stitches: Code B.

Within each category the stitches are placed in alphabetical order, and each stitch is coded so you can quickly recognize where it has been used in the houses portrayed in Part Three.

STITCH INSTRUCTIONS

The way to work each stitch is explained in diagram form, with numbers guiding you from the first to last steps of the stitch. Odd numbers indicate where the needle emerges to the upper side of the canvas; even numbers indicate where the needle is inserted to the underside. We also show a diagram of a completed area, to help you visualize how a stitch will look when worked up.

Following the working diagrams, we list the ways the stitch can be used in your design—for example, the Cashmere stitch (Code: D-1) can be used to depict window panes, door panels and garage doors.

STITCH VARIATIONS

The pattern and stitching variations with each stitch refer to the effects achieved when it is worked somewhat differently from the diagrams—worked vertically instead of horizontally, for example, which will usually alter the result remarkably. There is also a pronounced difference when the stitch placement is alternated in succeeding rows, which gives a less rigid appearance.

Random placement of stitches is another variation that is especially effective for the fluid edges of foliage. The random method can sometimes be used in combinations of stitches, or even with the same stitch worked in different sizes. If you have painted or color-marked the canvas, a less tight appearance can be achieved with this manner of working.

When a stitch may be worked "in a very random fashion," this means you can deviate from the diagram to suit your needs, and for an almost impressionist effect.

If, on the other hand, a stitch must be worked

"in an exact repeat pattern," this means that each part of the stitch must be worked in the same way as in the stitch before it—for example, the Cross stitches must all cross in exactly the same order.

The note on size variations will also tell you when a particular stitch can be enlarged by working across an additional number of threads.

Where the directions state that the stitch can be worked in any direction, this means you can start stitching on the left or right side, or at the bottom or top. When you have this choice, select the direction most comfortable for you.

Finally, we recognize that some people, especially accomplished needlepointers, will want to use a few stitches not found in this book or to invent their own; others will stick to our stitches but occasionally work them differently than we direct. For example, the oak tree's leaves on page 119 were done in the Leaf stitch (Code: L-11), but worked upside down to achieve a most interesting effect.

Now for the stitches. Most of the directions are based on the assumption that you are using size 13 or 14 Interlock canvas for your portrait, and that you will be stitching with medium tension.

ARCHITECTURAL DETAIL STITCHES

(Code: D)

These will create the important or significant architectural features in your picture, such as the windows and doors.

The detail stitches can be used alone or in conjunction with one of the basic Tent stitches (Code: B), and they can also be combined with each other. Many that are diagrammed in a vertical pattern can also be worked horizontally.

In the stitching, it is advisable to execute these small areas of detail stitches first, before putting in the surrounding larger areas. If you make a mistake in one of these vital details, you'll quickly spot it and easily correct it before any damage is done; the other area will fit in around any corrections you've made.

Since most detail stitches cover the canvas nicely, you do not have to paint the canvas under them unless you want to.

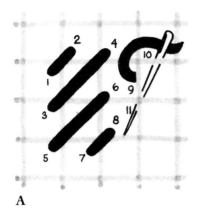

A

D-1
CASHMERE STITCH
Uses: rectangular window panes; door panels; paneled garage doors (diagrams A and B).

Pattern variations: can be placed horizontally or vertically.

Stitching variations: can slant to right or left; can be worked in any direction.

Size variations: can be enlarged in keeping with the pattern.

B 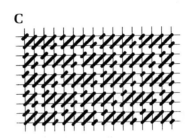   **C**   **D**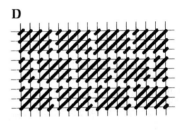

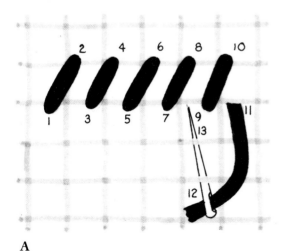

A

D-2
GOBELIN STITCH, SLANTED
Uses: louvered shutters, when worked across only two threads.

Pattern variations: none.

Stitching variations: can slant to right or left; can be worked in any direction.

Size variations: can be worked across as many threads as desired or necessary.

B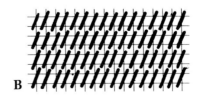

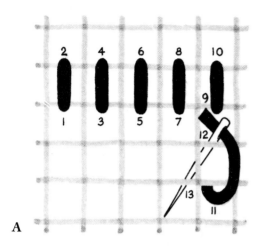

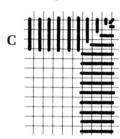

A   B   C

D-3

GOBELIN STITCH, STRAIGHT

Uses: smooth wood—doors, around doors, trim, beams, timbers, pillars, columns, plain shutters.

Pattern variations: can be placed horizontally or vertically.

Stitching variations: can be worked in any direction.

Size variations: can be worked across as many threads as desired or necessary.

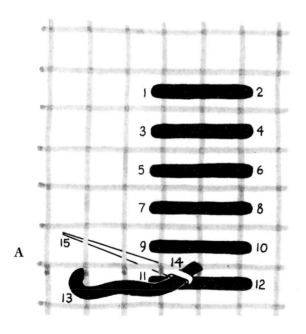

A

B

D-4

GOBELIN STITCH, STRAIGHT ENCROACHING

Uses: wood planked doors.

Pattern variations: can be placed horizontally or vertically.

Stitching variations: can be worked in any direction.

Size variations: can be worked across as many threads as desired or necessary.

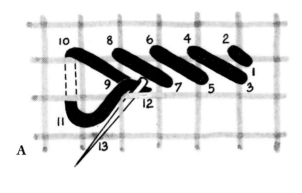

A

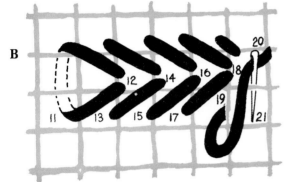

B

D-5

KALEM STITCH

Uses: louvered shutters, when worked horizontally (diagrams A, B, C).

Pattern variations: can be placed horizontally or vertically.

Stitching variations: can be worked in any direction.

Size variations: each complete stitch can be enlarged to go across as many threads as desired.

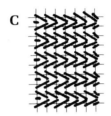

C

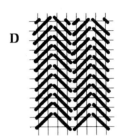

D

D-6

MOSAIC STITCH

Uses: small, square window panes.

Pattern variations: none.

Stitching variations: can slant to right or left.

Size variations: none.

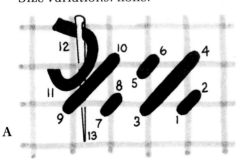

A

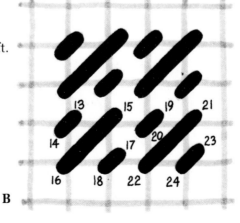

B

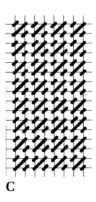

C

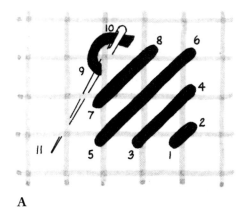

A

D-7

SCOTCH STITCH

Uses: small, square window panes; door panels.

Pattern variations: none.

Stitching variations: can slant to right or left; can be worked in any direction.

Size variations: can be enlarged in keeping with the square pattern.

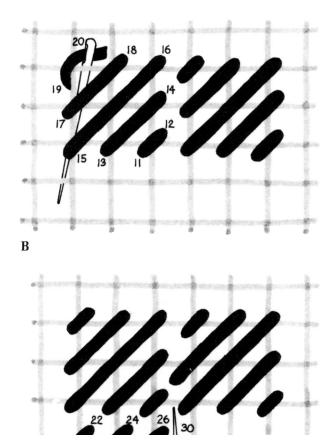

B

C

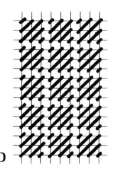

D

D-8

SPLIT STITCH

Uses: edging of prominent details, such as porch roof, doorway or cornice.

Pattern variations: none.

Stitching variations: can be worked in any direction, including diagonals and curves.

Size variations: can be worked tight or loose, depending on effect wanted.

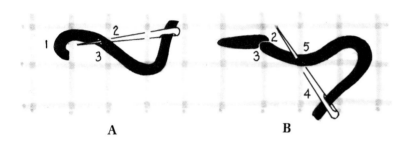

A   B

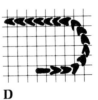

D

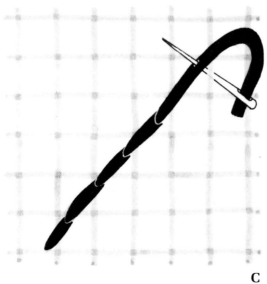

C

D-9

TENT STITCH, REVERSE ALTERNATING

Uses: louvered shutters.

Pattern variations: none.

Stitching variations: can be worked in any direction.

Size variations: none.

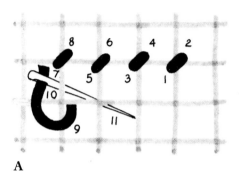

A

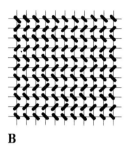

B

D-10

TRAMÉ, STRAIGHT GOBELIN

Uses: to give a fuller, more rounded effect to pillars or any projecting trim area.

Pattern variations: can be placed horizontally or vertically.

Stitching variations: can be worked in any direction.

Size variations: can be worked across as many threads as desired or necessary.

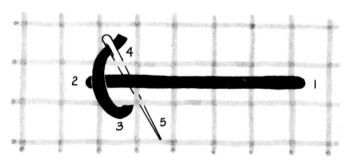

D-11

TRIANGLE STITCH

Uses: lower half of colonial style door.

Pattern variations: none.

Stitching variations: can be worked in any direction.

Size variations: can be enlarged in keeping with the pattern.

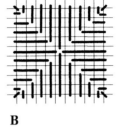

B

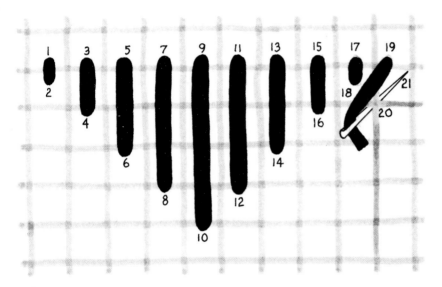

A

HOUSE STITCHES
(Code: H)

These are the stitches that represent various materials for house facades, such as brick, wood and stone, as well as the materials for roofs and edgings. Combinations of house stitches can be used for stonework composed of random sizes and textures. Sometimes you will want to choose a stitch with less accurate representa-tion in order to achieve a look of greater texture.

The house stitches will often have to be modified with some small stitches at the edges to fit the specified shape. They can also be aug-mented or used in combination with one of the Tent stitches. Because of such alterations, stitching should begin in an area to which the eye will be drawn first, most likely in the middle, around a door or other focal point.

You should work the roof of the house from the bottom to the top, because if you need extra threads for your stitchery to work out evenly, working up one or two more rows on the canvas will present no problem, whereas working down might. The precise, angled edges of the roof can be represented by using the Split stitch (Code: H-14) right over, or at the very edge of, the previously worked area. The Split stitch can also be used to portray curved lines more accurately, or strips of wood that cannot be represented in any other way.

The covering ability of the house stitches varies from stitch to stitch. Many of the straighter stitches give less coverage than the diagonal ones; therefore it is advisable to paint the canvas first if you select a straight stitch.

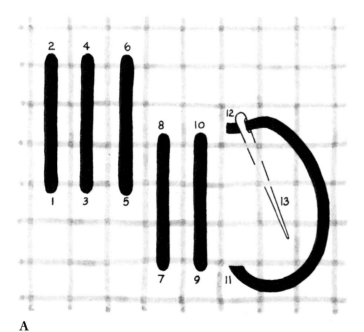

A

H-1
ALGERIAN STITCH

Uses: shingles; stone work.

Pattern variations: can be placed horizontally or vertically.

Stitching variations: can be worked in any direction.

Size variations: can span a desired even number of threads; can be widened or heightened across an even number of threads.

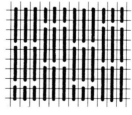

B

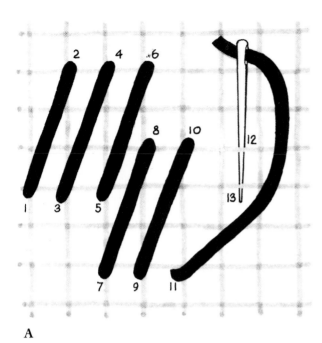

A

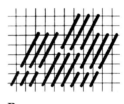

H-2

ALGERIAN STITCH, SLANTED

Uses: roof; wood shingles on three-quarter view of house.

Pattern variations: none.

Stitching variations: can slant to right or left.

Size variations: can be widened or heightened across an even number of threads.

B

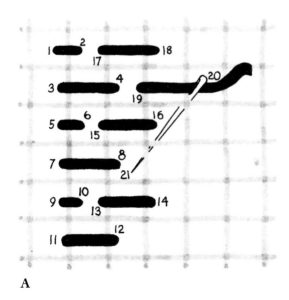

A

H-3

BRICK STITCH

Uses: brick; shingle or slate roof, when length is doubled (diagram B).

Pattern variations: can be placed horizontally or vertically.

Stitching variations: can be worked in any direction.

Size variations: can be doubled in size.

B

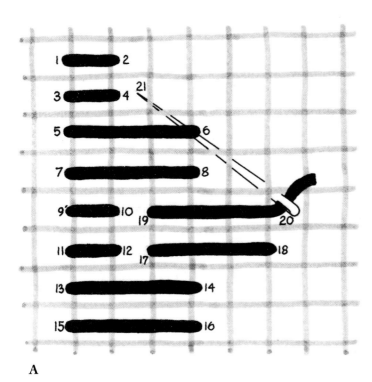

A

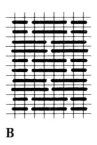

H-4
BRICK STITCH, DOUBLE
Uses: large brick; asphalt shingle or slate roof.
Pattern variations: can be placed horizontally or vertically.
Stitching variations: can be worked in any direction.
Size variations: none.

B

H-5
BUTTONHOLE STITCH
Uses: wooden strips that interrupt an otherwise smooth facade.
Pattern variations: can be placed horizontally or vertically.
Stitching variations: can be worked in any direction.
Size variations: can be worked across as many threads as desired or necessary.

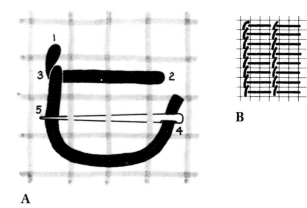

A

B

H-6
CASHMERE STITCH

Uses: slate roof, when worked horizontally across an even number of threads with each row alternating (diagrams C, D).

Pattern variations: can be placed horizontally or vertically.

Stitching variations: can slant to right or left; can be worked in any direction.

Size variations: can be enlarged in keeping with the pattern.

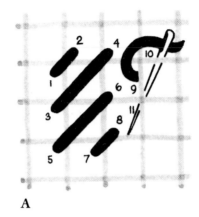

A

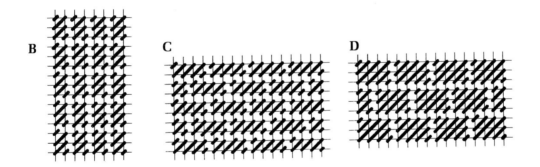

B   C   D

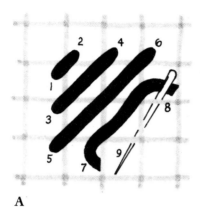

H-7
CHECKER STITCH
Uses: stone work.
Pattern variations: none.
Stitching variations: can slant to right or left; can be worked in any direction.
Size variations: can be enlarged in keeping with the pattern.

A

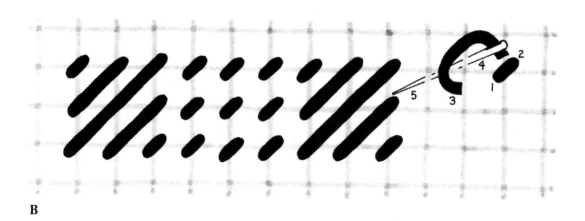

B

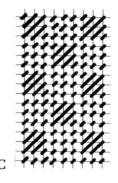

C

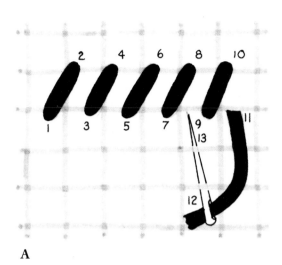

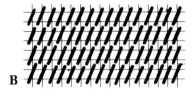

A

H-8
GOBELIN STITCH, SLANTED
Uses: clapboard siding; slate roof.
Pattern variations: none.
Stitching variations: can slant to right or left; can be worked in any direction.
Size variations: can be worked across as many threads as desired or necessary.

B

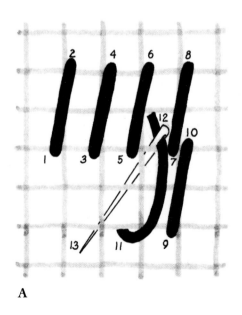

A

H-9
GOBELIN STITCH, SLANTED
   ENCROACHING
Uses: flat, uniform-looking shingles.
Pattern variations: none.
Stitching variations: can slant to right or left; can be worked in any direction.
Size variations: can be worked across as many threads as desired or necessary.

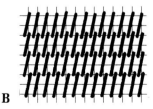

B

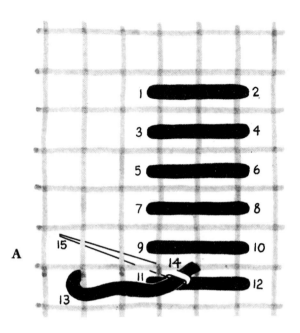

A

H-10

GOBELIN STITCH, STRAIGHT
    ENCROACHING

Uses: flat-surfaced wood planking; fences.

Pattern variations: can be placed horizontally
    or vertically.

Stitching variations: can be worked in any di-
    rection.

Size variations: can be worked across as many
    threads as desired or necessary.

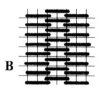

B

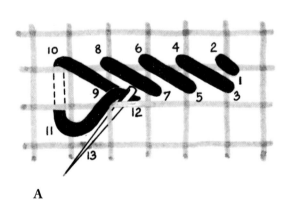

A

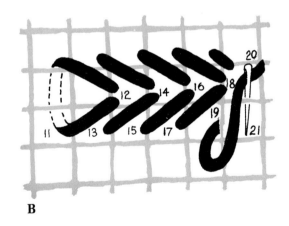

B

H-11

KALEM STITCH

Uses: herringbone brick, when worked ver-
    tically (diagram D).

Size variations: each complete stitch can be en-
    larged to go across as many threads as de-
    sired.

C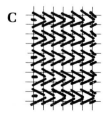

D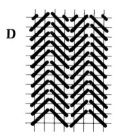

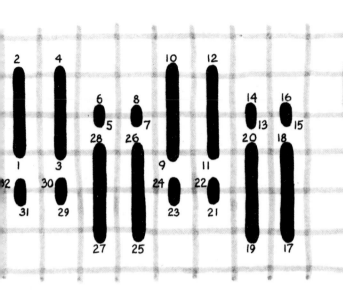

A

H-12
PARISIAN STITCH, DOUBLE
Uses: wood shingles on house or roof.
Pattern variations: can be placed horizontally or vertically.
Stitching variations: can be worked in any direction.
Size variations: can be enlarged in keeping with the pattern.

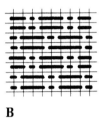

B

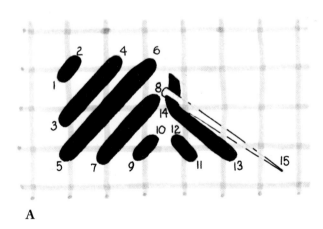

A

B

H-13
SCOTCH STITCH, ALTERNATING
Uses: shingled roof.
Pattern variations: none.
Stitching variations: can be worked in any direction.
Size variations: can be enlarged in keeping with the pattern.

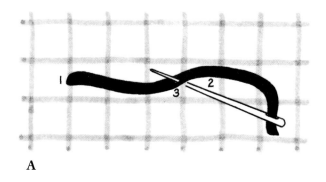

A

H-14
SPLIT STITCH, WIDE
Uses: angled wood trim; accenting decorative wooden trim or features; finishing off roof edges, or wherever a more pronounced line is desired.
Pattern variations: none.
Stitching variations: can be worked in any direction, including diagonals and curves.
Size variations: can be worked tight or loose, depending on effect wanted.

B

LANDSCAPE STITCHES
(Code: L)

Most landscape stitches are quite versatile in that they can be worked evenly with a set pattern, or they can alternate in placement, or they can be worked randomly; sizes and patterns can be mixed together, too. Many landscape stitches show up best when they are tweeded (see page 81), and all of them can be used in conjunction with one of the Tent stitches.

Do not stitch the foliage in your needlepoint portrait until you have completed the house. Trees shape up best when you begin stitching at the bottom of the green area and work up and out toward the top. Stitching on shrubs should begin at the top and work down, though you can stitch in from either side, if you prefer. A realistic portrayal of the irregular edges of trees and shrubs is achieved by breaking away from the stitch pattern. If a more forward appearance is desired for shrubbery, place a few threads at the top of the shrubs right over the house area.

Canvas underneath the landscape stitches should be painted, because the covering ability of these stitches varies. (Just remember to paint slightly within the outer edges, so the green underpainting doesn't extend to a pale surrounding area where it might show through.)

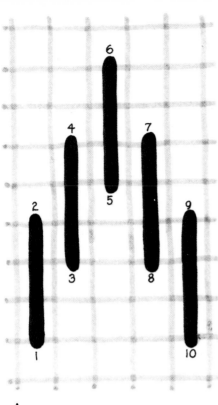

A

L-1
BARGELLO STITCH, RANDOM
Uses: shrubs; trees.
Pattern variations: only effective when worked in a completely random fashion; can be placed horizontally or vertically.
Stitching variations: can be worked in any direction.
Size variations: can be worked across as many threads as desired or necessary.

B

L-2
CROSS STITCH, DOUBLE STRAIGHT
Uses: shrubs; trees.
Pattern variations: can be placed evenly or randomly.
Stitching variations: crossing can be worked in exact repeat pattern or at random.
Size variations: can be doubled in size.

B

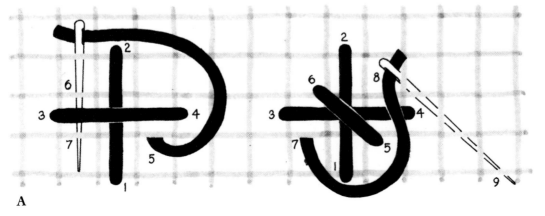

A

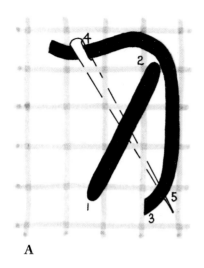

A

L-3

CROSS STITCH, OBLONG

Uses: shrubs; trees; bushes.

Pattern variations: can be placed horizontally or vertically; adapts well to being worked randomly.

Stitching variations; crossing can be worked in an exact repeat pattern or at random.

Size variations: can be worked across as many threads as desired or necessary.

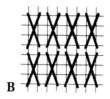

B

C

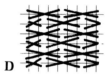

D

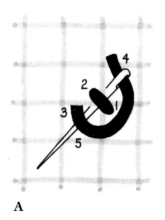

A

L-4

CROSS STITCH, PLAIN

Uses: shrubs with small leaves; patches of ivy; trailing vines.

Pattern variations: can be placed in even or alternating rows; adapts well to being worked randomly.

Stitching variations: crossing can be worked in an exact repeat pattern or at random.

Size variations: can be enlarged in both directions to go across as many threads as desired.

B

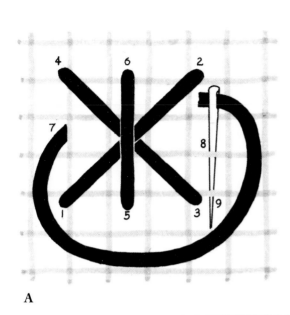

A

L-5

CROSS STITCH, SMYRNA

Uses: trees; shrubs.

Pattern variations: can be placed in even or alternating rows.

Stitching variations: crossing can be worked in an exact repeat pattern or at random.

Size variations: can be doubled in size.

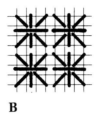

B

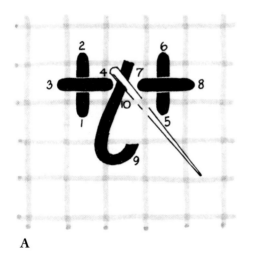

A

L-6

CROSS STITCH, UPRIGHT

Uses: bushes; shrubs; trees.

Pattern variations: adapts well to being worked randomly.

Stitching variations: can be worked in an exact repeat pattern or at random.

Size variations: can be worked across as many threads as desired or necessary.

B

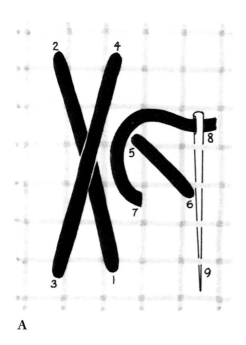

A

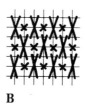

B

L-7
DOUBLE STITCH
Uses: shrubs with large leaves; hedges.
Pattern variations: can be placed horizontally or vertically.
Stitching variations: can be worked in any direction.
Size variations: can be doubled in size.

(*Opposite*)

L-8
HERRINGBONE STITCH, GONE WRONG
Uses: uniformly shaped hedges; evergreens.
Pattern variations: can be placed horizontally or vertically; edges may be altered to fit shape of shrubs by shortening or lengthening stitches.
Stitching variations: can be worked in any direction.
Size variations: can be worked across as many threads as desired or necessary.

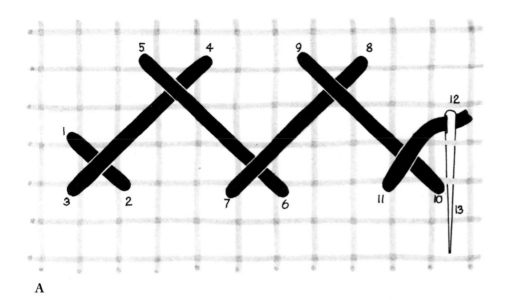

A

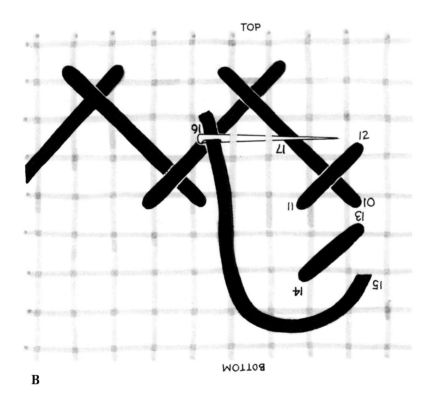

TOP

BOTTOM

B

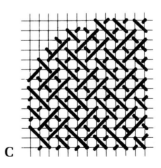

C

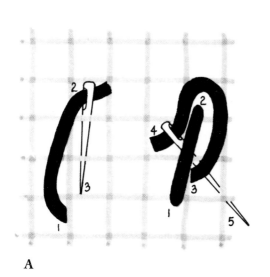

A

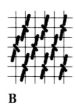

L-9

KNOTTED STITCH

Uses: bushes; trees.

Pattern variations: can be placed evenly or randomly; edges may be altered by angling the individual pattern diagonally or horizontally.

Stitching variations: can be worked in any direction.

Size variations: can be worked across as many threads as desired or necessary.

B

L-10

LEAF STITCH, MINI

Uses: twiggy looking bushes.

Pattern variations: can be placed evenly or randomly; edges may be altered by angling the individual pattern diagonally or horizontally.

Stitching variations: can be worked in any direction.

Size variations: can be worked across as many threads as desired or necessary.

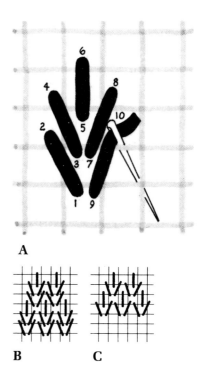

A

B   **C**

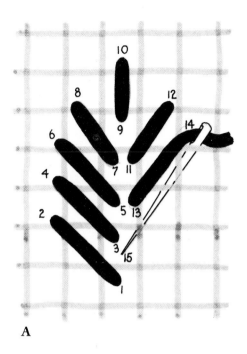

A

L-11
LEAF STITCH, SIMPLIFIED
Uses: trees.
Pattern variations: edges may be altered by angling the individual pattern diagonally or horizontally.
Stitching variations: can be worked in any direction.
Size variations: can be worked across as many threads as desired or necessary.

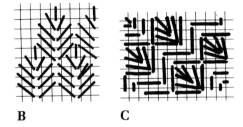

B   **C**

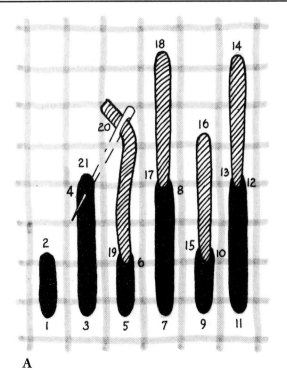

A

L-12
LONG AND SHORT STITCH
Uses: tree trunks.
Pattern variations: none.
Stitching variations: most effective when worked in a completely random fashion.
Size variations: can be worked across as many threads as desired or necessary.

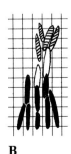

B

L-13

MOSAIC STITCH, DIAGONAL

Uses: to minimize shrubs or indicate them in
    background.

Pattern variations: none.

Stitching variations: can slant to right or to left.

Size variations: none.

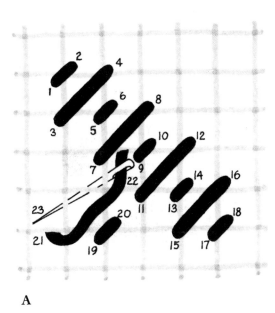

A

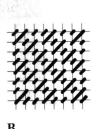

B

L-14

PLAITED STITCH

Uses: evergreen trees and shrubs.

Pattern variations: can be worked taller (diagrams A and B) or wider (diagrams C and D); can be placed horizontally or vertically; edges may be altered to fit shape of shrubs by shortening or lengthening stitches.

Stitching variations: most effective when worked in a very random fashion; can be worked in any direction.

Size variations: can be worked across as many threads as desired or necessary.

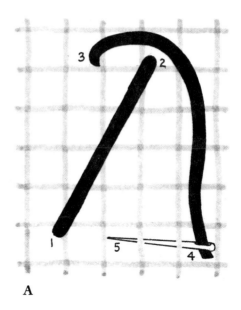

A

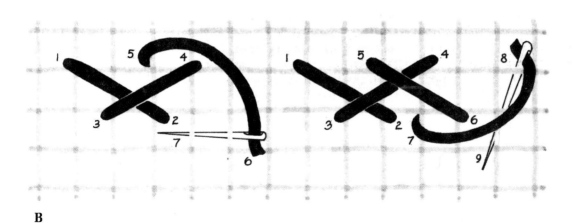

B

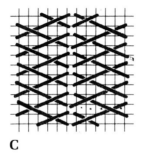

C

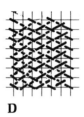

D

EMBROIDERY AND OVERLAY STITCHES
(Code: E)

Embroidery and overlay stitches are employed to represent those small items that are usually incidental to the basic design, such as doorknobs, door knockers, hanging baskets, flowers, lanterns and urns. These stitches should also be considered for any important details that cannot be worked with others without being completely lost in the finished picture. Another feature that works up best in embroidery is a fence or gate in front of the house.

Embroidery and overlay stitches are done right over a previously worked area and anchored to it. Thus, we recommend you finish all other stitching—including the background—before doing your embroidery and overlay work. In fact it's best to do it after blocking, so the embroidery lies correctly on the straightened canvas.

Using a new color, you can use the overlay technique to suggest shadows on shingles or a third color in a brick facade. Overlay can also modify certain shapes, such as a roof edge. It is nearly impossible to provide stitching directions for overlay work, because so much depends on where you decide to use it and the kind and thickness of thread you use. The color photographs of the finished needlepoint house portraits will show how we used them in all sorts of ways, and give you ideas for your own house.

E-1
CHAIN STITCH
Uses: detail work where a curved or straight line or other decorative effect is desired.
Pattern variations: none.
Stitching variations: can be worked in any direction.
Size variations: can be enlarged in keeping with the pattern.

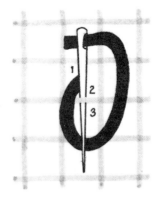

A

B

C

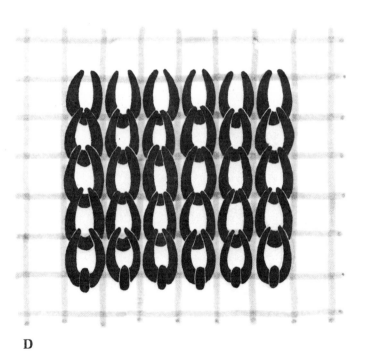

D

E-2

FRENCH KNOT STITCH

Uses: flower blossoms.

Pattern variations: none.

Stitching variations: none. (See placement across canvas threads, diagrams A, B and C, or as overlay embroidery, diagram D.)

Size variations: can be enlarged by additional twists over needle, or by using multiple threads.

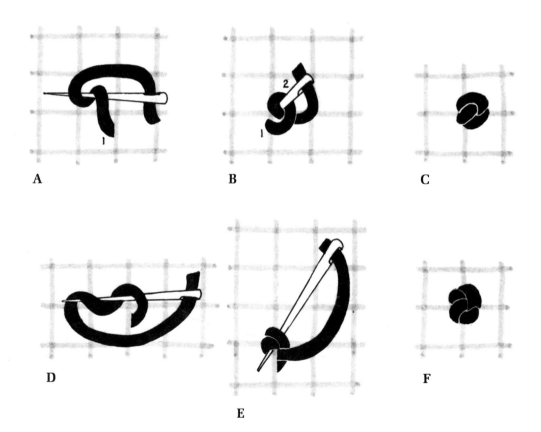

A   B   C

D   F

E

E-3

OVERLAY WORK

Uses: details such as doorknobs, window pane divisions, fences and fluted columns.

Pattern variations: always anchored to a pre-worked area, pulled up and through the work and laid over it in the desired pattern. (See the finished needlepoint house portraits for various uses.)

A

E-4

LAZY DAISY STITCH

Uses: delicate, lacy leaves.

Pattern variations: effective only when placed in a completely random fashion.

Stitching variations: can be worked in any direction.

Size variations: can be worked in any size.

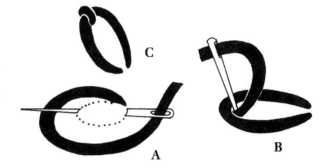

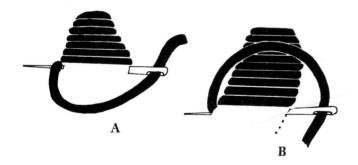

A

B

E-5

SATIN STITCH

Uses: any small area with a smooth surface.

Pattern variations: can adapt to any shape.

Stitching variations: can be worked in any direction.

Size variations: can be worked in any size.

THE BASIC BACKGROUND STITCHES
(Code: B)

These are the three Tent stitches: Basketweave, Continental and Half Cross—all of them diagonal stitches worked across a single thread of canvas; they can be slanted to the right or to the left. Although extremely versatile and easy to work, the Tent stitches should be used sparingly on a needlepoint house portrait, because they do not project adequate textural interest by themselves. Thus, solitary Tent stitches are best suited for the background and for small detail areas. On the other hand, when Tent stitches are used in combination with other stitches, they take on a freshness and importance they rarely possess on their own, and this is how you will often employ them.

As we suggested earlier, the background should be secondary to the textured house, therefore it's best to work your background Tent stitches with a single thread of yarn.

Before deciding which Tent stitch to use, study the advantages and disadvantages listed for each one. Though they look alike on the surface of the canvas, each is worked differently and has its own limitations. However, one advantage may outweigh several disadvantages—for instance, if you have a large area to cover, Basketweave is your best stitch (despite its disadvantages) because it is easily worked and holds the canvas in shape. On the other hand, if you have a small, irregular area, Continental is best despite its tendency to distort the canvas. And the Half Cross, which doesn't cover the canvas as well and is rather awkward to work, can be the right stitch if you have a single line to fill.

B-1
BASKETWEAVE (TENT) STITCH

Advantages: keeps canvas in shape; can be worked on all types of canvas; canvas does not need to be turned when working; covers adequately with a single thread.

Disadvantages: difficult to use in small areas; cannot be used for single rows; must be worked diagonally; difficult to rip out.

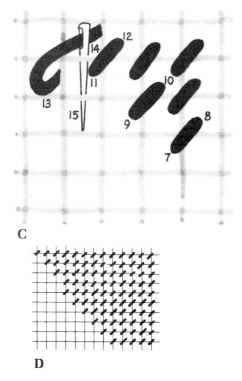

C

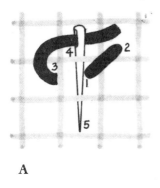

A

B

D

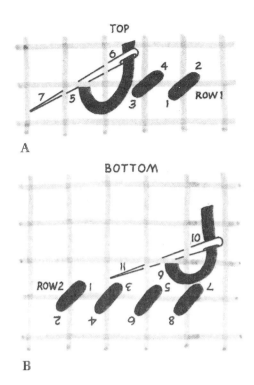

A

B

B-2

CONTINENTAL (TENT) STITCH

Advantages: can be worked in any direction; very maneuverable for small, irregular areas; can be used for single diagonal, vertical or horizontal lines; can be used on all types of canvas; covers adequately with a single thread.

Disadvantages: twists canvas out of shape; work must be turned upside down at the start of each successive row.

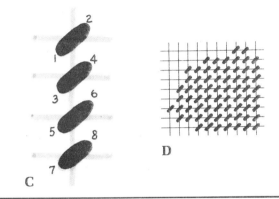

C

D

B-3

HALF CROSS (TENT) STITCH

Advantages: keeps canvas in relatively straight shape; can be used for single rows; can be worked horizontally or vertically; uses less yarn than the other Tent stitches; works up to be thinner than the other Tent stitches.

Disadvantages: can be used only on Interlock mono (or penelope) canvas; hard to achieve a smooth working rhythm, because of closeness of emerging and inserting points; somewhat difficult to use in small, irregular areas; not suited to working with a single thread.

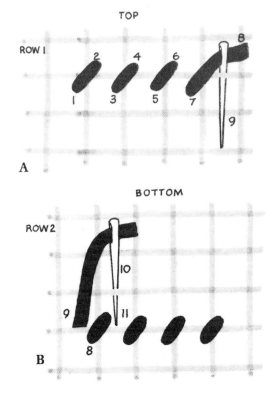

A

B

7. Stitching Techniques and Tips

For those of you who have done needlepoint before, this chapter may appear worthy of only a superficial glance. But we think this information is essential to needlepoint novice and expert alike, because needlepoint houses are very special, and these tips will be useful to you.

The best stitching of your own house will depend on a number of variables, the first of which is the yarn.

THE YARN

YARN COLOR

Obviously, you know the colors of the house you're going to portray—your house in needlepoint—and you will want to duplicate those colors as closely as possible. But when you are ready to buy the yarn, you may be disappointed in the choice of colors available at your local needlework or craft shop. Although some large shops carry four or more shades of a single color, they are the exception rather than the rule; and in any case, none of the shades you find may be exactly what you need.

When you cannot find yarn in the exact color, you'll have to buy a color that comes closest to it. However, if the area to be stitched is not a solid color but irregular, or composed of several colors (as with brick and stone), you should be able to achieve a realistic look by tweeding and shading, as described later on in this chapter.

HOW MUCH YARN TO BUY

Most of your needlepoint portraits will be stitched in Persian yarn, each strand of which measures about 1 yard (90 cm.) and consists of three intertwining threads. You will use two of these three threads together when stitching, so reserve the third thread and use it later with a thread from another strand.

One yard of the two yarn threads will usually cover about 1 square inch (2.5 square cm.) of canvas when stitched, but the amount of coverage can vary according to the stitch being worked. For example, certain basic stitches like the Basketweave (Code: B-1) take more yarn than, say, the Brick stitch (Code: H-3), and decorative overlay stitches usually take the least amount of yarn.

Before buying yarn for your needlepoint portrait, measure the areas of different colors on the marked or painted canvas in order to estimate roughly how much of each color you will need. Then if you are still in doubt about quantity, take the canvas with you to the shop and ask the salesperson for advice.

It is wise to buy a little more yarn than you think you'll need for your portrait. If you don't buy enough and have to return for more, you may find the color is slightly different in the new batch, because it comes from another dye lot, or it may be sold out altogether. If you buy too much yarn and return the excess within a reasonable time, you will probably be given credit or be able to make a fair exchange. Truly small amounts of leftover yarn can be used up eventually on other needlepoint projects.

HOW LONG A THREAD TO WORK WITH

The length of working yarn is usually determined by the stitch. Generally speaking, you can use a longer length of yarn, up to a full strand, for a stitch that covers several threads of canvas, whereas you should use a shorter length, 20 to 30 inches (50 to 75 cm.), for a stitch worked across only one or two canvas threads. This is because the yarn tends to fuzz and thin out from constant pulling through the meshes.

If your canvas is the recommended size 13 or 14 Interlock Mono, you will be executing most of the stitches with two threads of a strand of Persian yarn. There will be exceptions when you use one thread or three, but usually only for embroidered details and the background area.

STARTING THE WORK

THREADING THE NEEDLE

The needle can be threaded in one of two ways. You can thread it as you would for conventional hand sewing, though this isn't easy to do. The best way is to fold the end of the yarn tightly over the pointed end of the needle, then withdraw the needle, still holding the folded yarn tightly between thumb and forefinger. Ease the eye of the needle over the tight fold, and then you'll be able to pull it through. Whichever method you use, don't knot the yarn.

BEGINNING AND ENDING-OFF STITCHING

Start by coming up from the underside of the canvas with the yarn and pull it through, leaving a 1 inch (2.5 cm.) tail underneath; hold the tail under the canvas with your free hand in the path of your work and catch it down as you execute the first few stitches. This starting procedure locks the end of the yarn and the first stitches solidly in place.

When you have almost used up a piece of yarn, end it off on the underside by pulling the remaining yarn back through the last few stitches you've worked, then cut it off very close.

THE ORDER OF WORK

Always start with the architectural details—windows, shutters, doors, pillars, porches, etcetera. Then fill in the facade of the house around these details. Work the roof next (from bottom to top, as described on page 56), adding accents and trim as needed.

When the house is completed, start on the landscaping (see page 64). When landscaping is done, fill in the background—and remember to work this with a single thread of yarn (see page 78), or double if your portrait will be subject to wear.

Last of all, do the embroidery and overlay stitches—doorknobs, flowers, fences and so on—that are always placed on top of other finished areas.

SPECIAL TECHNIQUES

TWEEDING

Tweeding is combining two threads of yarn of different colors, working the two threads as one. In a sense, you are doing what the artist does when he mixes two colors of paint together. But unlike the artist who creates a completely new color in this way, you will obtain a tweeded look as the two yarns combine in different ways in different parts of your stitch.

Tweeding is one of your biggest assets in striving for a realistic representation of your house in needlepoint. Though it should not be overdone, tweeding makes possible more accurate treatment of such features as brick, stone, stucco, shingles, and slate roofs—in short, things that are composed of several colors and have interesting textures. Since these features often cover large areas of the canvas, it is important that the colors be as close to reality as possible. Study a particular area to be tweeded before deciding on your yarn colors—for example, is the stonework beige and gray, or beige and white? Is the brick red and pink, or red and orange? Are the shingles brown and black, or brown and gray? Frequently you'll find those features composed of different colors than you thought.

Where appropriate, you can vary tweeding by laying over it some threads in a third color. For example, if you have tweeded a shade of tan and rust to achieve the color of a brick facade, you can overlay the stitches with some dark brown threads in a random fashion to define a few of the bricks (as in the color workups shown on pages 26-27). You will see other examples of tweeding in the color photographs in Part Three. Here, too, we advise you to experiment with tweeding on scraps of canvas before deciding which color combinations will work best for your own house in needlepoint.

A final note on tweeding: in order to achieve unexpected colorations, which is the true charm of tweeding, pay no attention to the position of the two yarn colors as they are stitched.

SHADING
Shading is a variation of tweeding, but uses tones of the same color.

Shading is almost mandatory for the execution of foliage, since no real-life tree or shrub is ever a single shade of green; rather, each is a fascinating combination of shifting green lights and shadows. Three shades of green yarn (light, medium and dark) will produce six variations of green—solid light green, solid medium green, solid dark green, tweeded light and medium green, tweeded medium and dark green, tweeded light and dark green. With these variations of color—and texture, too—you can approximate the appearance of foliage.

Certain stitches lend themselves better than others to the tweeding and shading techniques. Experiment with your chosen stitches and colors to make sure.

TWO-SIZE CANVAS TECHNIQUE
Some houses have small but extremely important areas of very small detail, such as a stained glass window. If you have such an area, you might consider working it separately on petit point canvas with a single thread of yarn, leaving a 1 inch (2.5 cm.) unworked canvas border around the edge of the stitching.

Then place the detail on the right side of your mono canvas—baste it down with buttonhole thread, or put a few dabs of white glue on the mono canvas, place the detail in position and weight it down until the glue is dry.

There will be more threads to the petit point canvas, and they should be woven into the surrounding mono canvas. Unravel the unworked petit point canvas threads around the detail and weave them into the mono canvas, ending all threads on the underside.

Immediately work one or two rows of stitching close around the detail—working right through the mono canvas and interwoven detail threads—to lock your detail in place. One of the Tent stitches (Codes B-1, B-2, B-3) is best for this. Follow the detail outlines closely, making sure to leave no unworked canvas threads around it.

ADDITIONAL STITCHING TIPS

1) When you are going from one area of a color to another of the same color, and you must

cross an unworked area that will be worked in a completely different color, you must end-off your work and start afresh with the new area.

Do not be tempted to carry your piece of yarn underneath the unworked area—for when you are working it later you are likely to catch up some of the underneath yarn and it will show on the right side of your portrait.

However, when you are working a large area composed of several shades of a basic color (as with a slate roof), you can carry your yarn underneath from one small area to another without worry. (Otherwise you'd constantly be rethreading your needle.) Note the roofs on the English Tudor and Georgian Colonial houses in Chapters 11 and 12 for examples of the kind of area we mean.

2) Your needlepoint house must be worked at a medium tension. If you make the mistake of pulling your yarn too tightly while stitching— and many needlepointers tend to do this—it will not cover well and the canvas will show through the picture after it is blocked.

3) If your yarn twists as you are stitching, simply drop the needle from the underside of the canvas and let it hang while the thread untwists before you resume stitching.

4) We recommend you use the Basketweave (Code: B-1) or Half Cross stitch (Code: B-3) for any large area instead of the more familiar Continental stitch (Code: B-2), because the Continental tends to distort the canvas when it is worked over a large area.

5) When working a complex stitch, try to keep in mind the shape and pattern of the finished stitch; this will help make it more familiar and easy to execute.

6) When you make a mistake over a small area, pick out the stitches one at a time with the end of your needle. If the area is large, rip out the stitches with embroidery scissors or a seam ripper, which is an inexpensive tool available in fabric and sewing shops.

The only difficult stitches to rip out are the tight ones, such as the Tent stitches. Be extremely careful in ripping them out to avoid cutting the threads of your canvas. If you should accidentally cut them, baste a patch of the same canvas behind the cut, and proceed to stitch through the two layers of canvas as if they were one.

7) If stitching becomes monotonous at times, especially when working on a large house, we recommend you skip around from one area to another—but only after the doors and windows have been stitched. In other words, if it bores you on a particular day to keep working on a brown tree trunk, switch over to stitching flowers with embroidery floss. Of course, you must always keep the general order of your design in mind when you do this.

8) Most needlepoint house portraits will not require a frame, but if yours is oversize, you may want to construct a simple frame to hold the canvas in shape while working on it. Use strips of pine firring 1 inch wide and ¼ inch thick purchased from your local lumberyard and cut to the size of your canvas. Nail the frame together at the four corners, and tack the canvas along the edges of the frame with upholstery tacks. Such a frame was built for the Georgian Colonial house in Chapter 11 and cost much less than a dollar.

When working with a frame you must support it on the two arms of a chair, or else weight down one end of the frame on a table or desk, letting the rest of the frame and canvas hang over the edge so you can work on it unencumbered. A frame makes your canvas pretty difficult to move around, and it also requires you to keep one hand under the canvas all the time, but these disadvantages are outweighed by the fact that your canvas will not twist out of shape. Once you have completed stitching except for the background, you should remove the canvas from the frame to work the background, which would take much longer to do on the frame with one hand always under the canvas.

9) To avoid an unwieldy canvas, roll up the part you're not working on and secure the rolled-up portion at both ends with paper clips or hair clips. It's a good idea to protect the roll from getting soiled by wrapping cheesecloth around it.

Three

YOUR HOUSE
IN NEEDLEPOINT

In this part you will find ten houses, including a town schoolhouse, that have all been stitched in needlepoint, each an impressive example of the realism, originality and beauty possible with this unique form of portraiture.

The houses in these chapters highlight most of the design and stitching problems you will encounter with your own house, whatever its architectural period—and we discuss them all and show you how we solved them.

For each house, we show the original black-and-white snapshot, the chart that grew from it (together with the stitch codes for each part), and, in full color, the completed needlepoint portrait—so you can see exactly how the colors and stitches were used to achieve texture and definition.

We hope they will be your chief source of ideas and inspiration, to refer to again and again as you portray your own house in needlepoint.

8. Colonial House

This house in the Colonial style is typical of many built in the United States after World War II, when the major emphasis in housing was on efficiency. Situated on a small level lot on a quiet side street, the house was easy to photograph for the needlepoint portrait.

The tree on the right was reduced in height and brought in closer to the house, while the tree directly in front of the house was eliminated. Because the lines of the house are tailored, the landscaping was purposely treated in the same way.

The appearance of a cloud and bird in the sky not only helps balance the composition, it adds a natural—and somewhat whimsical—note to the picture.

DESIGN CONSIDERATIONS

The most pressing design problem was to portray the three very different textures of the facade—shingle, stone, and brick—when they were all painted the same shade of white. The stitch representing the stonework on the lower half of the facade was not as realistic as it could have been, but this was done deliberately so as not to interfere with the stitch for the brick chimney. In other words, a more accurate stitch for the stonework would have made the chimney appear less forward and would have detracted from the importance of this central feature in the design of the house. For the same reason, the entire chimney was treated as brick—though in reality the botton half is stone—so the bottom half would not melt into the surrounding stone facade. The shingles of the upper facade are also merely suggested instead of being precisely duplicated, which is in keeping with the tidy appearance of the house.

The wood-paneled garage door was minimized in width, since it is actually slightly recessed from the front of the house, and was given a stitch that represents it perfectly but still does not call undue attention to the area. A second-floor projection over the entry roof on the back of the house was eliminated completely because it was unimportant to the representation of the house.

STITCHING CONSIDERATIONS

The all-white facade made it difficult to visualize where one stitch began and another ended. Thus, it was necessary to complete the chim-

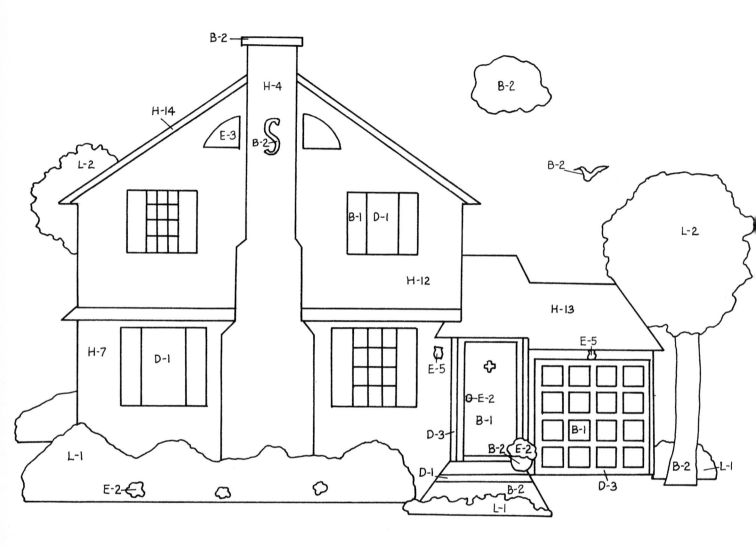

ney right after the windows had been put in before the rest of the facade was stitched. By doing so, other details in relation to the chimney could be seen easily.

The edge of the roof was emphasized with a stitch worked in a different color, with three threads of yarn being used instead of the usual two; the chimney top was defined in the same way.

The shrubbery was given dimension by using a solid dark color at the bottom, progressing up to a medium light tweed, and capping the shrubs with a solid light color.

Because the house was predominantly white, it was felt that the background color should provide greater contrast than usual. The choice was a deep tan executed in the Continental stitch with a single thread of yarn.

COLONIAL
12 x 16 inches (30 x 40 cm.)

9. Contemporary House

This striking contemporary house is a fine example of the custom-built home, whether it be ranch, bi-level, tri-level, or any other modern plan with Colonial overtones.

Most of the design problems with this shingle-and-brick house were caused by the long sweeping lines of its facade. In fact, the length of the house made it impossible to be in front of all parts of the house at one time. Therefore, the owner had to stand across the street on a neighbor's property in order to get a workable snapshot. A tree in the neighbor's yard appears in the snapshot, but naturally was eliminated in the needlepoint composition. A slightly three-quarter view of the dormer windows is evident in the photograph but was ignored in the design. The chimney, however, was portrayed as it appears in the photograph—at an angle—to give the design some dimension.

In spite of the problems it posed, the length of the house was an important architectural feature, and the owner wanted the finished portrait to reflect this. The solution was to use a long, narrow piece of canvas, which minimized space above and below the house and helped dramatize its length. Of course, this meant that a stock-sized picture frame had to be ruled out.

It was decided to reduce the size of the trees in the back of the property and to introduce a non-existent tree on the right at the point where the property falls off toward a heavily wooded section in the rear; similarly, the grassy area in front was made to drop off to the right. These alterations help balance the composition.

DESIGN CONSIDERATIONS

This house presented a number of problems because of its length and its many areas of detail. The first problem to be resolved was the size and number of windows in relation to the shape of the house. In order to keep the house from being overly long, it was decided to make the window panes as small as possible though each one of them would be represented.

To begin the design, the house was divided into three sections: the center, the right, and the left. The size of the windows in the right section was determined first, as was the space between them. Then the exterior lines of this side of the house were put in. Next, the center section's lower roof line was added, and within this shape, the dormer windows were inserted.

The left section was put in last because it was the least interesting from a design standpoint.

The doorway area, with its paneled door and narrow windows, demanded careful attention to work in the number of threads required by the stitches for this area. In effect, the stitches finally determined the area's proportion.

The center window, which projects but is not a true bay window, was put in the space between the left section of the house and the front door. The stitch used to represent this window made it larger than it is in reality, a deliberate move because the window is an interesting detail that should be played up and because it was known the window would provide a neutral background for the flowering cherry tree to be embroidered over it later.

The length of the house's center section was reduced slightly to minimize the heaviness of the roof. Yet the detail features of this section fit in so nicely that the proportion looks accurate, although in fact it is not.

STITCHING CONSIDERATIONS

The shake shingles on the facade were executed in the Straight Gobelin stitch; then to give the appearance of rough edges and shadows, a darker color was overlaid at random, occasionally encroaching on the next row of shingles. Overlay embroidery was used on the roof, too, with the darker gray applied over the lighter gray after the latter had been stitched. The center section of the roof was set apart from the two side sections by using the Split stitch at the section's edges.

The vertical ridged planking to the right of the door was done with a single thread of yarn to prevent it from becoming overly thick and prominent. Though the planking, the window shutters and trim are all stark white in reality, these areas were stitched in an off-white color so the white wrought-iron railing would show up; the railing was added on later with embroidery floss available only in one shade of white, a pure white.

The flowering cherry tree and the red maple tree were embroidered over the previously worked areas underneath them. The blossoms of the cherry tree were worked in embroidery floss to highlight their delicacy, as were the white blossoms of the bush on the far left. The leaves of the red maple were executed with a single thread of yarn with little attention paid to whether they were actually attached to the tree's branches; again, this was done to create a look of lightness. Both the cherry and red maple trees were merely suggested so as not to block out much of the facade of the house.

The color for the background of the picture presented a real problem because of the preponderance of shades of green in the portrait. The original choice was a very pale green, but when the stitching of the house and landscape had been completed and some pale green yarn was held up to the canvas, a real loss of color occurred. Next, an off-white was considered, but quickly rejected because of the large amount of white already in the picture. The color finally decided upon was the palest shade of gold available—it was the only workable color because of the many varied shades of colors in the portrait.

CONTEMPORARY
9½ x 21 inches (23.75 x 52.5 cm.)

Pattern for this contemporary house will be found on pages 94-95.

10. Dutch Colonial House

This gracious sixty-year-old Dutch Colonial house, with its authentic gambrel roof and clapboard-and-shingle facade, is an honest adaptation of its ancestor. Because it sits on a very wide street and there were no trees in the front yard, it was exceptionally easy to photograph.

The owner of the house has portrayed it in needlepoint twice, with a time span of four years between the first and second portrayals. The second portrayal was prompted by a repainting of the house. The first portrayal was charted with the help of a simple drawing while the second portrayal was scaled up from a photograph, which is why the second rendition is far more realistic.

FIRST PORTRAIT

DESIGN CONSIDERATIONS

In this version the owner decided to play up the house and its unusually large, eight-over-eight pane windows and to minimize the setting.

While the roof line of the house in the first portrait is representative, it is not entirely accurate in its proportion because the second-floor dormer windows were designed to be the same size as the first-floor windows, whereas in reality the latter are larger.

The window trim was eliminated because it was white like the facade, and consequently was deemed unimportant. Likewise, the wood paneling around the door was treated very simply because it was white.

The front steps were increased in width as they descended to achieve perspective; while the actual number of steps was not accurately portrayed.

The large tree on the left was placed closer to the house than it actually is, although its massive foliage in the design mirrors reality.

The background was left unfinished in order to lend dimension to the project, highlight the house, and give the picture the look of antique needlepoint.

STITCHING CONSIDERATIONS

The entire house was executed with very simple stitches, which all but ignore the many textures of the facade. The shrubbery and the tree were also treated simply; all the shrubs,

except for the one on the far right, were done in the same stitch. A solid color was used at the base of the foliage while tweeding was employed at the top.

SECOND PORTRAIT

DESIGN CONSIDERATIONS

In the second portrait the house is almost as long as in the first but not as tall; this is because the owner decided to emphasize the woodland setting as much as the house, because the foliage provides an interesting contrast in color and texture. But not all the trees could be shown because they would swamp the house; furthermore, the three trees incorporated into the design had to be greatly reduced in height.

Notice the reduction of the tree behind the sun porch; in part, it was included to soften the harsh roof line, but it had to be shortened, or it would have appeared to be growing right out of the roof.

The second-floor dormer windows were made smaller than they actually are to make the proportions of the roof-and-dormer area seem more accurate. To help show the projection of this area, the white trim across the top of the dormer window area was put in. The curvature on the sides of the roof—not even shown in the first portrayal—was not only made important but exaggerated slightly in the design.

An accurate representation of the wood paneling around the door necessitated a careful counting of threads for the stitches to execute

Chart for Dutch Colonial first portrait

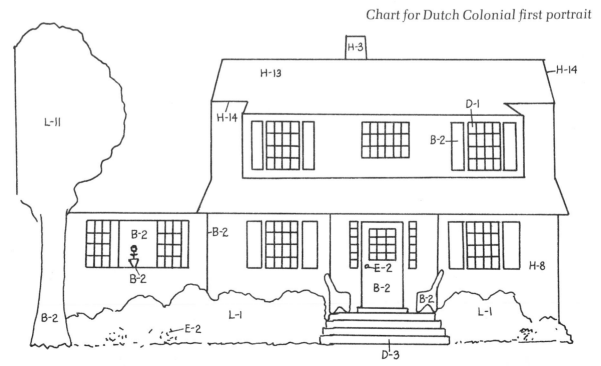

DUTCH COLONIAL
16 x 20 inches (40 x 50 cm.)

*Chart for Dutch Colonial second portrait
is overleaf, page 101*

it. The white trim on the windows to either side of the door was included in the second portrayal because it offers a good contrast to the gold facade.

The sun porch was deliberately set off from the rest of the house by a single row of a different stitch.

The inclusion of a lower set of steps and the bushes alongside it reinforces perspective and helps show that the house sits on a slight knoll; this is emphasized further by the sloping off of the grassy area.

STITCHING CONSIDERATIONS

Instead of being stitched like the facade of the lower half of the house, the facade of the dormer window area was executed in a stitch to give the appearance of shingles. After the wood paneling around the door was stitched, the benches on either side were executed in a stitch that projects them.

Stitches for trees and shrubs were chosen for a lot of color and textural contrast and were worked very randomly. The center tree was given dark shadows with overlay threads. The trunk of the tree on the left was tweeded in black and dark brown to simulate ridges of bark.

The background was stitched with a single thread of white yarn.

COMPARISON OF THE TWO PORTRAITS

A study of the simple, almost primitive first portrait and the more detailed, sophisticated second version reveals the variations that can exist in two approaches to the design and stitching of the same subject matter.

The first portrait lacks detail and is inaccurate in its proportions because it was based on a sketch rather than a snapshot; also, when the owner designed it she wanted the picture to be simple. Four years later she had acquired a lot of design and needlework experience, and the second version—with its accurate proportions and wealth of detail—reflects this.

A more finished look was desired for the background in the second portrait. After experimenting with various background treatments, the owner decided on the use of a single thread of yarn, which acts to subdue the background and thrust the house forward; this is an extremely satisfactory treatment for most needlepoint house projects.

We are not recommending either one of these needlepoint portraits over the other. We think they are both wonderful, and leave it up to you as to which approach you prefer.

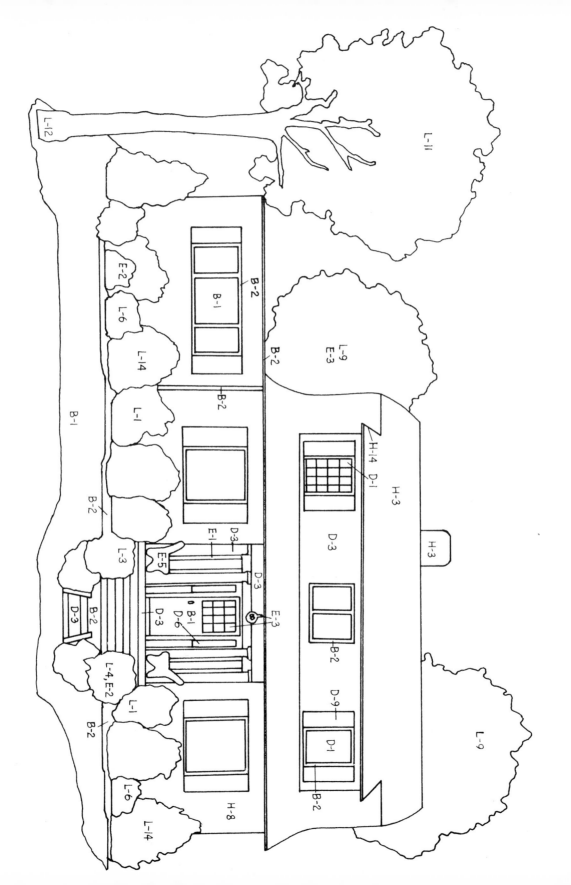

11. English Tudor House

The English Tudor house with a handsome her-ringbone-brick-and-stucco facade crisscrossed by weathered timbers sits on a lot almost as attractive as the house. For this reason the owner wanted to stress the lush green setting as much as the house in the needlepoint portrait.

Photographing the house posed no problems because most of the trees, except for the two in front of the house, are on the sides or at the back of the property. The two front trees were kept in the picture because they are an integral part of the landscape, but their foliage was moved up and minimized so it would not block the herringbone brick of the facade; also, they were designed to run off the canvas in order to indicate their tremendous height. The row of tall evergreens along the front of the house was lowered in height and filled in where sparse.

DESIGN CONSIDERATIONS

In many of these portraits the size of the house on canvas is determined by the number and size of the windows. This house is ususual in that its size was determined by the herringbone brick pattern on the facade, which the owner felt was the most distinguishing feature. The windows were considered secondary because they were few in number and would look fine in whatever size they worked out to be in rela-tion to the brick facade. It was also decided to execute the windows' leaded partitions in over-lay embroidery with dark green heavy-duty thread.

After much experimentation the Kalem stitch was selected to best represent the herringbone brick pattern; then to get the measurements for the total brick area, the number of threads was counted out for each angled pattern of the brick as well as the timbers. Next, the threads for the stucco areas and the windows were counted so the exterior lines of the house could be drawn; certain minor adjustments had to be made later, but at least that created a framework to begin filling in. The peaked area of the gable on the left side of the house was drawn in next.

Because the surrounding trees were so large, they threatened to overwhelm the house unless treated very airily, which was what the owner decided to do.

STITCHING CONSIDERATIONS

An interesting stitching procedure was used

ENGLISH TUDOR
14 x 20 inches (35 x 50 cm.)

for the angled timber on the left side of the house. A base of Continental stitches was put in first, and on top of this a row of covering stitches, which are the only ones that show—this was necessary because otherwise it would have been impossible to stitch the angled timber evenly.

The slate roof has many colors ranging from off-white to black, with many shades of gray in between. Working this on the horizontal required jumping from place to place with a particular color of yarn, counting up and across each time before beginning in a new area; because the distances were short and all the roof colors somewhat similar, it did not hurt to carry the threads across the back of the canvas.

The planked oak door was worked with a single thread in a stitch chosen to prevent the door from projecting too much and interfering with the facade.

The evergreens across the front of the house were tweeded with light and dark green yarn, using the same stitch but working it randomly to achieve interesting light and shadow effects as well as perspective. The leaves of the trees were also worked randomly with wide spaces between stitches. The two large tree trunks in front of the house were executed in oversized stitches to give them importance.

The background was stitched after the leaves—not an easy task because it required stitching in a previously worked and rather tight area, but the pleasing effect was worth the trouble.

L-4

12. Georgian Colonial House

This brick house in the Georgian style is distinguished by its formality and symmetry, as evidenced in the careful placement of the windows and chimneys, by the wrought-iron gates, and by the meticulous attention to details like the dentil molding and doorway paneling.

Because the house is unusually large in relation to its grounds and because adjacent homes crowd in, it was not possible to obtain one shot of the whole house (the snapshot you see here was taken with a wide-angled lens). So the owner had to take three separate shots from roughly the same distance and piece them together.

A separate charting had to be done for the center section of the wrought-iron gates in order to render the elaborate, intricate detail work. Eventually, the gates were made smaller than they are in reality in order to minimize their prominence but still give them the attention they deserve.

A large tree which is actually in front of the house was eliminated, because it covered a good part of the facade. But other trees were included, although they were positioned differently than they really are, in order to soften the house's lines. Most of the shrubbery bordering the property was omitted, too, except for the two large azaleas beside the wrought-iron gates.

GEORGIAN COLONIAL
16 x 26 inches (40 x 65 cm.)

DESIGN CONSIDERATIONS

Before planning could proceed, the best representation for the wrought-iron gates had to be figured out, so they would be played up but at the same time not blanket the center of the house. This was achieved by portraying the gates from a viewpoint slightly above them, while the house is viewed head on; although this is not entirely accurate, the combination of the two views works most effectively. It was also decided to double the size of the bricks in the gate pillars, though in reality they are the same size as the bricks in the house—this improves the perspective, making the gates appear to be out in front, which they are.

Once the problem of the gates was solved, there was the equally challenging problem of scaling up the extraordinary number of windows, which were all kept because they are an integral part of the architectural style. Since all the window panes were the same size, the number of threads needed for each pane was counted out and then each window was placed in the design. After that the house and roof lines could be established.

The elaborate paneled doorway, flanked by Corinthian columns and topped by a broken pediment, was represented very simply because of the overlay embroidery which would be added later for the wrought-iron gates. The length of the house made it possible to accurately represent the dentil molding just below the roof line, which was fortunate because it's an important detail of this house; gray was alternated with white to simulate the molding.

Because the chimneys rising from the center section are also significant features, it was decided to show all four of them in an exaggerated three-quarter perspective.

The trees and shrubs were designed to be simple and precise in keeping with the architecture of the house. The shape of the lawn was dictated by the gates, which the lawn had to incorporate and emphasize.

STITCHING CONSIDERATIONS

After much trial and error, the colors selected for the facade were dusty pink and light tan; these were tweeded together to portray the lovely pink-brown color of handmade James River, Virginia, brick.

The slate roof was also portrayed as realistically as possible with three different shades of gray and a muted purple introduced occasionally. A rather unusual stitching technique was used for the roof: this consisted of working several stitches in one color and then jumping away a short distance and continuing with the same color in another area. This meant carrying the yarn across the back of the canvas, which was all right because all the roof colors are similar. If the Slanted or Straight Gobelin stitches are used, this method of stitching goes very quickly and requires relatively little counting when jumping from spot to spot. Another way to handle the roof would be to have several needles threaded with the different colors and work much as you do with bobbins when knitting argyle socks; this eliminates having to carry yarn across the back of the canvas.

The pineapple finials on top of the brick gate pillars were accentuated with crisscross overlay threads and a Chain stitch curving around the middle. The wrought-iron portions of the gates were not put in until all the work underneath—including the lawn—had been completed. Embroidery floss was used for the wrought iron, to simulate its hard and shiny appearance and to make the intricate embroidery detail work easier to execute. The embroidery was begun in the center and worked out toward the edges, while paying very close atten-

tion to the separate design chart for the gates.

The background was stitched with the neutral putty color to make the house stand out dramatically. A white background was ruled out because of the white trim on the house.

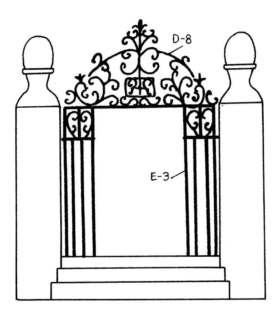

Chart for complete Georgian Colonial house will be found on pages 110-111

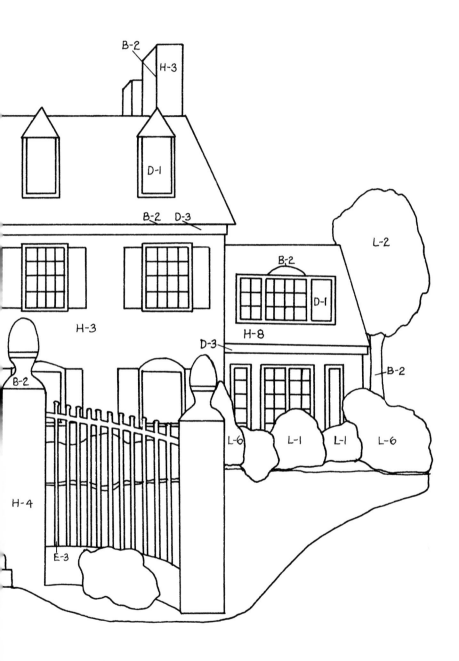

13. Town Schoolhouse

Some people will be interested in portraying other places besides their house—a church, courthouse, school, town hall, office building or historical landmark. For this reason we have included a one-room schoolhouse in Florham Park, New Jersey, which is listed in the national and state registers of historical sites. The brick-and-wood-shingle building was erected in 1866.

The schoolhouse portrait is a departure in other ways, too. First, it was scaled up from a pen-and-ink drawing printed on a calendar. Second, instead of being portrayed head on, it presents us with a three-quarter view, which is the only practical way to see the main building's extensions. Finally, a background of blue sky and a foreground of grass were stitched in to give a scenic quality.

Today the schoolhouse sits in the middle of a commercial district, so the surroundings were idealized to make them look as they must have many years ago.

DESIGN CONSIDERATIONS

Any three-quarter view presents the problem of representing the angle changes within the limi- tations posed by the strictly vertical and horizontal lines of the canvas. To put it another way, you are constantly forced to straighten lines that in reality would be falling away from the horizontal. The problem of perspective with the schoolhouse was solved, to a large extent, by making the panes of the two windows on the right larger than those on the left, though in reality all panes are the same size. Because of this trick, the right-hand windows appear to be more forward in the picture than the others.

The top edge of the roof was the only line angled accurately to show perspective; this was possible because nothing except the cupola depended on that line. The cupola was shortened in keeping with the project's small dimensions.

The front doors had to be designed head on instead of falling away as they do in reality, but the treatment of the two roof overhangs helped suggest some perspective. Again because of the straight canvas lines, the shed-like extension in back lacks perspective, but its true angles were suggested by a judicious positioning of shrubbery, which also diverts attention from the inaccurate perspective lines.

Inner and outer corner angles were empha-

sized with a single row of Continental stitches. Note the inclusion of a drainpipe to define the front corner—such details should be eliminated unless serving a useful purpose, as the drainpipe does here.

STITCHING CONSIDERATIONS

The old brick of the schoolhouse facade was tweeded in a deep red and pink-tan; the dark and light colors together help suggest the appearance of brick and mortar.

The roof overhangs were emphasized by outlining them with the Split stitch. The right sides of the overhangs were done in Tent stitches slanting to the left to follow the slope of the roof.

Because the shed on the left is entirely white, the defining corner line had to be stitched first in order to visualize how the rest of the area would fit in; all other aspects of the shed fell into place around this line.

The background and foreground colors were chosen to simulate sky and grass. Although this might seem quite logical, it does present certain problems. First, it is impossible to duplicate the true colors of sky and grass. The sky here was executed with a single thread of pale blue yarn, which makes it look lighter and airier than it would in two threads. The second problem is deciding where the sky should meet the grass without adding numerous details to define the horizon, which are only possible when the house sits in a wide open space. Without these details the eye is drawn to the abrupt and unrealistic merger of sky and grass instead of to the main attraction—in this case, the schoolhouse.

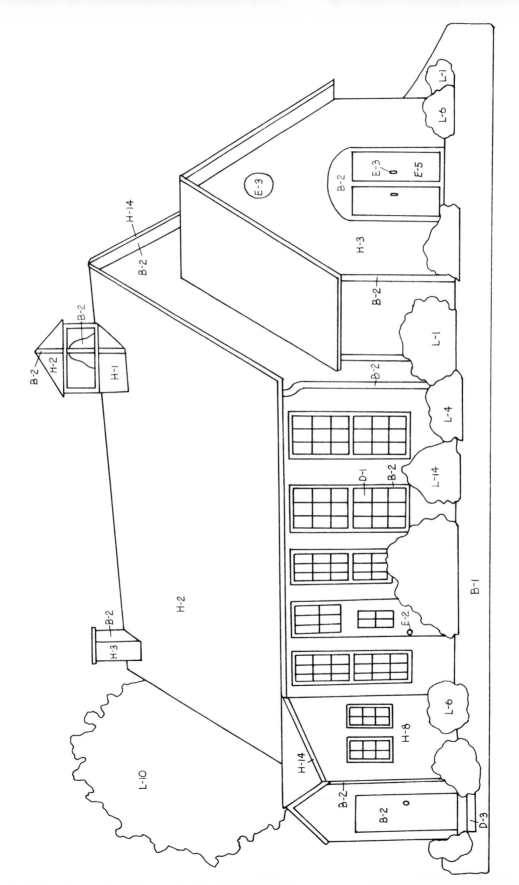

TOWN SCHOOLHOUSE
12 x 18 inches (30 x 45 cm.)

14. Turn-of-the-Century House

The mint condition of this older house in its manicured setting is reflected in the careful execution of its needlepoint portrait.

It was necessary to take two snapshots of the house. The first was the head-on view the owner wanted to portray, but because a large tree directly in front partially obscures this view, a second was taken at an angle to capture certain details more clearly. Thus, a combination of the two snapshots was used in the charting.

The curved hedges along the walk leading up to the house were shortened and modified to bring them into the design, while the rest of the foliage was altered only slightly. The walk, which also leads to a rear garden, helps draw your eye into the heart of the picture.

DESIGN CONSIDERATIONS

The owner, an avid gardener, loved the setting as much as the house itself, so she included every aspect of the setting except the tree out in front—this meant foliage, gateposts, sidewalk, flowers and flower boxes. Fortunately the size of the finished portrait did not matter, which allowed a great deal of flexibility in the design.

In this house, it's the porch that's centered, rather than the front door, so the porch was the starting point of the design. After it was in, the other roof lines were placed in relation to it.

An extension on the second floor on the right side was eliminated because it confused the design by appearing too much in the foreground.

The white window trim was considered important because of the large expanses of glass in the rather plain windows. To keep the trim from bleeding into the equally white clapboard facade, the shutters were elongated.

The two hedges flanking the walk were executed in a darker green at the bottom and a lighter at the top. This two-tone treatment, along with the small section of sidewalk showing near the gateposts, helps the eye distinguish between them.

STITCHING CONSIDERATIONS

Interesting and unusual color variations in the trees were achieved by the use of blocks of light and dark green. These blocks of color were tweeded on the tree at the left, but on the large

oak tree they were done in Leaf stitch worked upside down to give the leaves a rather droopy appearance. The shrubs were stitched in a very exact fashion, letting the many different colors and shapes suggest their variety. The grass was purposely worked in an unconventional stitch to lend weight and emphasis to the lower half of the picture.

The background was worked with a single thread of pale blue yarn, but not to resemble the sky—instead, it was chosen to coordinate with the colors of the room in which the picture would hang. The single thread of yarn reduces the intensity of the color and achieves an almost gossamer effect that makes the house and setting stand out all the more. This method works up more quickly because the single thread goes through the meshes of the canvas more easily, but if you work with a single thread, be sure not to work too tightly.

Chart and color photographs overleaf

TURN-OF-THE-CENTURY
16 x 24 inches (40 x 60 cm.)

15. Victorian House

Typical of the architecture of the late nineteenth century, this delightful house is pure Victoriana with its clapboard facade, elongated windows, and gingerbread trim. Whether or not you live in a Victorian house, you may want to portray a similar structure in needlepoint as a fitting memento of a bygone era. The Victorian house can be depicted in a variety of colors and trims, and if desired, the roof can be flattened into a mansard.

This Victorian house is typically tall and narrow, which was the feature the owner wanted to play up. This was accomplished by severely minimizing the setting, which, although attractive, consists of an abundance of foliage that practically obliterates the house. Leaving out all but a few shrubs in front dictated a tall and narrow picture which in turn helped emphasize the tall, narrow lines of the house. However, this particular portrait could certainly be squared off by adding a few trees on either side.

Photographing the house proved to be a real problem because of the density of trees and the heavily traveled street in front of it. The solution was to photograph it in the winter and on a Sunday. It was shot as close up as possible so as to record all the marvelous Victorian details.

It was decided to leave the canvas background unfinished, but to stitch a border around the edge to resemble a mat; the burgundy yarn used for this was a favorite Victorian color and provides a lovely contrast to the gold clapboard facade of the house.

DESIGN CONSIDERATIONS

Although a tall and narrow house was desired, it had to be large enough to show the characteristic Victorian details like the molding and gin-

VICTORIAN
15 x 17 inches (37.5 x 42.5 cm.)

gerbread trim. Unfortunately, this also meant highlighting the broad expanses of glass in the Victorian windows.

The porch was the next design consideration because of its fancy trim, which was to be overlaid later, and the number of its supporting pillars. The pillars on the far right were made shorter and thinner as they recede to indicate perspective and to show that the porch wraps around the side of the house. Another touch that gives it depth is the triangular area of gray stitching under the porch roof on the right.

After the porch pillars were drawn in, the first-floor windows were positioned in relation to them. Space was left between the tops of these windows and the porch roof trim for the wooden crosspiece that joins the pieces of gingerbread trim to each other.

The windows were easy to position because only their shapes had to be considered.

STITCHING CONSIDERATIONS

The windows were stitched in a darker gray than is normally used, because the neutral color of the trim required a greater contrast than a pale gray would have provided. The darker gray is a good choice, too, for large, unbroken expanses of glass for it helps make them appear to recede.

The trim on the peaked section beneath the roof was made more accurate by slanting the Continental stitches on the left side toward the right and slanting the stitches on the right toward the left. The Split stitch was used for the protruding roof line above the trim. The dentil molding below the trim was executed with single thread overlays. The same treatment was used along the roof edge of the porch. The short pieces of horizontal dentil molding on the second floor were defined with gray yarn to give a shadow effect, necessary because the areas are so small.

The clapboard facade underneath the porch overhang was stitched in a darker shade of gold than the facade above the porch to indicate that it is in the shadow of the porch. The very narrow strip of facade to the left of the porch was tweeded with the darker gold used beneath the porch and the lighter gold used above it; this achieved a better blend where the two sections meet.

The gingerbread trim was executed with overlay embroidery and French knots, using two threads of yarn in the same color as the pillars and roof trim.

The texture of the stitch chosen for the burgundy border contrasts nicely with the stark background of unfinished canvas. The stitches met at right angles at the four corners to create the effect of a mitered mat.

16. Other Houses and Details

We wish we had the space to include completed needlepoint portraits for every conceivable kind of house and house detail that might be of interest to our readers. Obviously this is not possible, but we can present a few more examples of needlepoint house portraits to serve as inspiration and help you solve problems that may not have been covered in the preceding chapters.

BACK VIEW OF A NORMAN FRENCH HOUSE

The back view of this magnificent house in the Norman French style is definitely the better one to portray in needlepoint. In addition to the advantages of beautiful foliage, flower-dotted terrace and gay striped awnings, this side of the house is also where the family spends most of its time during warm weather, so this view means a great deal to them. In reality there is also a swimming pool which could have been included if a more casual portrait had been desired. See photograph above, opposite.

Because the brick facade is white and the slate roof a pale gray, the only possible color for the window panes was a very dark gray. The striped awnings, shown rolled up, were given an appealing texture by stitching them with two double threads overlaid horizontally in the darker color and then lashing them in place with short, single vertical threads in the lighter color. Like all overlay embroidery, they were put in after all other stitching was completed.

The center section of the house protrudes, and to indicate this the edges were stitched in a single row of Continental stitches.

The stockade fence was represented accurately by the Kalem stitch tweeded in beige and brown yarn.

The gray slates of the patio were given definition and perspective by overlaying some dark gray threads.

ATTACHED ROW HOUSE

A house that is part of a row of houses, such as you often find in cities, can be treated in one of two ways. One way is to portray it along with the houses on either side; with this approach we suggest you stitch the adjacent houses in shades of gray that eventually fade into the background color or the edge of the canvas.

Another way is to treat it as if it existed independently of neighboring houses—this is the treatment used on the brick-and-stucco house shown here, which is a typical English row house. See photograph below, opposite.

ADDITIONAL ARCHITECTURAL AND LANDSCAPE DETAIL

Though the houses in Part Three represent a wide range of popular architectural styles and decorative details, as well as landscaping, here are some other unusual features and combinations of features that may occur in your house and pose problems in your needlepoint portrait.

PROTRUDING PORCH

One way to treat a protruding porch is to completely darken the recessive area, perhaps working in a few overlay threads to give vague definition to doors or windows. Another treatment is to give the protruding porch a more prominent stitch than the recessive area, and in addition work the recessive area in a slightly darker shade.

Protruding porch

Tile roof

TILE ROOF

The tiles on a roof can be rounded or angled, but the shape is not as important as the correct color choice. A possible treatment for a tile roof is suggested visually in the color photograph on page 27. Individual tiles can be defined by the use of dark overlay threads.

Screened porch

SCREENED PORCH

Screening can never look completely realistic in needlepoint. However, for a large area of screening such as a porch, select a medium shade of gray (making sure it is darker than the windows) and with a single thread of yarn, work one of the Tent stitches to achieve a gossamer, almost see-through effect.

House with jalousies

JALOUSIES

Jalousies on windows can be stitched as solid glass in the Continental stitch with overlay threads added later to define the individual panes of glass. Or the jalousies can be executed with rows of Straight Gobelin stitch or an elongated Cashmere stitch. Jalousied doors should be treated as solid glass.

TURRET
Any curved shape on a house is handled best
by suggesting the curve at the bottom roof edge
with a curving Split stitch.

Turret

Broken facade

BROKEN FACADE
Angle changes in a facade, such as the jutting out of a bay window, require definition at the break points. This can be handled with single rows of the Continental or Split stitch.

Large expanse of glass

LARGE EXPANSES OF GLASS
Glass walls and oversized picture windows can be treated very simply with the Continental stitch, but make sure you add some textural interest to the area around the glass.

Four

BLOCKING AND FINISHING

17. Blocking the Canvas

As you stitched your needlepoint portrait, chances are the canvas pulled somewhat out of line, depending on the stitches you used. Some distort the canvas considerably; others hardly at all. To return the canvas to its original shape, it is necessary to block it.

Certain pieces of needlepoint require very little blocking; others need major help. In general, larger pieces of needlepoint need more blocking than smaller pieces, and your own stitching technique will also help determine the amount of blocking needed.

Actually, we believe every portrait should be blocked, even those that appear to be in great shape. Blocking gives a professional finish that cannot be achieved any other way, and after all the time and thought spent on a portrait, it seems a shame not to give it the very best look possible.

Your choice of blocking method depends on the degree to which your canvas has been distorted, and on whether the stitches are flat or textured.

THE IRONING BOARD METHOD

If you have used flat stitches, and if your portrait is more rumpled than misshapen, the ironing board method of blocking is favored. Place an old bath towel on a padded ironing board, then place your needlepoint portrait on it, right side up. Cover it with a clean damp cloth—preferably thin cotton or cheesecloth—and steam press it with the iron set at "wool." Press very lightly, setting the iron down in one area and lifting it up completely, then moving on to the next area. When the entire canvas is smoothed out, pin the corners and edges in place with rust-proof thumb tacks or T-pins and let dry for twelve hours, checking periodically to see that it doesn't shift out of position.

The ironing board method is also used when the main outlines of the canvas are fine, but there are a few misshapen areas, such as doors or windows that are off the straight. Each one will require special attention as you press, then pull it carefully back into shape. To do this, hold the iron just above (not on) the detail, wait until the canvas is pliant from the steam, and then start pinning around the distorted area with rust-proof straight pins, beginning at the corners and working in; use as many pins as necessary to obtain the correct shape. Work each detail in this manner, and when you are finished, pin down the edges of the house and of the canvas and let dry.

DAMP BLOCKING

Canvases with a lot of texture in the stitches should not be pressed or the textures will be flattened down. Instead they should be damp blocked in one of two ways, depending on the amount of distortion.

For this you will need a flat surface larger than your canvas, on which to pin it. A drawing board, fiberboard, wallboard or soft pine board are all good—and you can often find scraps of the right size at a lumber yard or building supplies store. First thing is to mark the board with horizontal and vertical guidelines for your blocking. Or you can cover the board with checked gingham, carefully lined up with the edges of the board, and tightly tacked underneath, which will also give you true horizontal and vertical lines to follow.

FOR CANVASES ONLY SLIGHTLY OUT OF SHAPE

Place your canvas right side up on the board, making sure it is lined up with the horizontal and vertical guidelines. Starting in the upper right-hand corner, staple the unworked edge of the canvas all the way down the right side with a open stapler or staple gun. (Staple only in the unworked canvas, never through completed needlepoint.) Staples should be 1 or 2 inches (2.5 or 5 cm.) apart, depending on the degree of hold required. Then staple across the top of the canvas, pulling firmly to make it smooth. Next, work down the left side and across the bottom from the right, alternating as you go, and pulling firmly to line up the canvas threads with the guidelines on the board.

Now take a piece of medium weight cloth (an old sheet, dish towel or T-shirt) big enough to cover your canvas, and completely saturate it with cold water. Wring it out until it is not quite dripping wet and lay it over the portrait,

pressing down and smoothing out with your hands. Leave the cloth on for twelve to twenty-four hours, or until cloth and portrait are completely dry. The portrait can easily be removed from the board by pulling the staples straight up with fingers or a screwdriver.

FOR BADLY DISTORTED CANVASES

Put the canvas on your blocking board right side up. Mist the canvas with water dispensed from a plant mister, atomizer or ironing sprinkler—do not soak the canvas, just mist enough to dampen the needlepoint and the canvas without saturating. Next, wet the unworked edges of the canvas with a damp sponge. Begin to pull and stretch the canvas up, down and on the diagonal until you can pin the four corners in their correct positions with rust-proof tacks or T-pins. When the corners are secured, place tacks opposite each other in the middle of the four edges and work out to the corners, putting in more tacks 1 inch apart. Keep tacking up and down opposite sides, always in the unworked canvas border. When the canvas is pinned into shape, lightly mist it again and let it dry thoroughly over several days so there is no danger of its getting distorted again.

You can always have your canvas professionally blocked, but this is expensive, and besides, you can never be sure the canvas won't be dipped in water as part of the blocking procedure. We advocate professional blocking only if you know and trust the people doing it, or if they have an excellent reputation for this sort of work.

18. Framing and Other Finishing Touches

FRAMING

FINDING YOUR FRAME

The easiest, quickest and cheapest way to obtain a frame is to buy one in a stock size from a frame shop, art or craft supplies shop or mail-order catalog. They come in a number of sizes suitable for these needlepoint portraits. The most popular are: 12 x 16″ (30 x 40 cm.), 16 x 20″ (40 x 50 cm.) and 18 x 24″ (45 x 60 cm.). If you have planned the dimensions of your portrait to fit a ready-made frame, you will have little trouble picking it out. These frames are available in many finishes, or you can buy them unfinished and stain or paint in the color of your choice.

You can also buy a secondhand or antique frame and refinish it. The search for such a frame will undoubtedly take longer and you may end up spending more money, but your reward will be a more unusual and valuable frame, usually of superior workmanship.

Whether you opt for an old or new frame, it should never draw attention away from the needlepoint it surrounds. Thus, you should avoid frames with gilt or elaborate carving—in fact, it is better to choose a frame that is too plain rather than one verging on the ornate. Whether it is stained or painted depends on what best complements your portrait. Of course a frame should fit into the room where it will hang—you would not place a very ornate frame in a simply furnished room. As a rule of thumb, select a frame that is not faddish but will wear well over a long period of time, for your needlepoint portrait is likely to become a family heirloom.

The proportions of the frame should be right for the picture. An otherwise flawless job can be ruined if a small picture is set in a big hulking frame, yet people often make this mistake. The frame should not call attention to itself—its purpose is to set off your needlepoint. For portraits measuring up to 20 x 24″ (50 x 60 cm.) the frame should be no wider than 1 to 1¾″ (2.5 to 4.5 cm.).

Finally, you should check the construction of the frame very carefully. Look at the corners to determine if they are fastened together soundly. They should be mitered at an exact 45-degree angle and put together with glue and nails with no gaps between the mitered parts.

If the frame is old and you want to use it as is, check the surface to make certain it is smooth.

However, if you are going to refinish it, or it is a new unfinished frame, you can take it home and sand it if it seems a bit rough. After sanding, apply a sealer or primer, and then apply paint or stain. If you're painting it, wait until the first coat is thoroughly dry, then give it a second coat. If you're staining, wait until the stain is dry, then rub the frame with #0000 steel wool before applying one coat of varnish or two coats of shellac. Use the steel wool again between the two coats; let everything dry thoroughly between and after them.

GLASS OR NO GLASS?

Your framed needlepoint portraits look most inviting without glass covering them. However, if you want to protect them, you have a choice of regular or non-glare glass. The advantage of the latter is that reflection is minimized, allowing you to see the needlepoint more closely. However, non-glare glass has a tendency to flatten textures, and it is much more expensive than regular glass.

Stock-size frames come complete with either kind of glass. For other frames, you can buy the glass at a hardware store or from your local framer and have it cut to the size you need.

BACKING YOUR CANVAS FOR FRAMING

Before framing your portrait, you need to mount it on something stiff enough to hold it taut inside the frame. Heavy cardboard, called backing board, is available at art supply and stationery stores. (You can also use Masonite, if you have it; plywood or other wood is very heavy for hanging.)

The backing board should be cut a bit smaller than the frame to allow for the thickness of the canvas mounted around it. Center the portrait carefully on the backing board, wrapping the unworked canvas edges around to the back. (Hold them with masking tape as you check for position.)

When the portrait is perfectly centered, staple or glue the canvas edges to the back of your board. If you're using glue, be sure it is white resin glue, and do one edge at a time, letting it dry thoroughly before going on to the next. (The remaining edges will be held by the masking tape until you're ready to glue them.)

If you're using a mat (see below), you can cut the backing board to exact size to fit the frame, and staple or glue your canvas directly to the front of the board, as the mat will cover the unfinished edges.

MAKING A MAT

A mat can be fitted around your needlepoint portrait—for the sake of appearance, or to enlarge it to fit a particular frame, or both. Construct the mat out of heavy mat board purchased at an art supply store, where you will find it in a wide range of pleasing colors.

Cut the exterior dimensions of the mat to fit into the frame, and then cut out a center section to form a window for your needlepoint picture. For the cutting you will need a metal-edged ruler and a craft knife or a single-edged razor blade.

You can also make a less expensive mat in much the same way by cutting a cardboard gift box to fit into the frame, and cutting out the window. Then cover the mat with adhesive-backed paper in a burlap, linen or other texture.

DOING THE FRAMING

When everything is ready, assemble as follows: first insert the glass, if you're using it. Then insert the mat. Next comes the needlepoint portrait mounted on its backing board. When everything is in place, tack a few tiny headless nails into both inner sides of the frame in back, letting them extend out sideways over the backing board to hold everything securely in place.

If you like, the entire back can be covered with a sheet of brown wrapping paper. It should be cut to come just within the outer edges of the frame. The easiest way to attach it is with masking tape, or you can also glue it in place with white glue.

Last of all, attach screw eyes and picture wire to the back of the frame, and your needlepoint portrait is ready for hanging.

HANGING YOUR FRAMED PORTRAIT

Portraits up to 20 x 24″ (50 x 60 cm.) should be hung at eye level. Larger portraits should be hung slightly above eye level, but no higher.

PROTECTING YOUR PORTRAIT

Unless it's hung under glass, your portrait will get dusty, so occasionally you should brush it lightly with a clean whisk broom or vacuum it gently with a low-power or car vacuum cleaner. If the needlepoint becomes lightly soiled, sponge very gently with the suds from some cold water liquid soap mixed according to the directions on the bottle. Do not apply the mixture, just the suds, then clean off the suds with a cloth that has been wrung out in clean water. If your needlepoint becomes badly soiled, have it dry cleaned. Do *not* attempt to wash it in cold or warm water.

KNIFE-EDGED PILLOW

If your needlepoint portrait is going to be finished as a pillow, you need to stitch a few additional outer rows of the background stitch for a seam allowance; this will give the canvas strength and prevent the edges from raveling. Next, buy a pillow form made out of Dacron,

foam rubber or kapok. You will also need approximately one-half yard (45 cm.) of backing fabric in heavy cotton, velveteen or corduroy; you may need additional fabric if it is narrow, or if you plan to make your own cording.

CORDING

You can buy it ready-made in the color of your choice, or you can make your own to match the backing. Either way you'll need about 5 feet of cording for a 14″ pillow. When measuring, remember to allow a few extra inches for going around corners and for beginning and ending off.

To make your own cording: cut 2″ bias strips of your backing fabric. Cut as many strips as needed and seam them together (on the straight of the goods) to make a long continuous strip of bias. Press the seams out flat. Lay the cord in the center of the bias strip, fold the strip over and stitch as close to the cord as possible (use the zipper foot for this).

To attach the cording to the pillow: Baste the cording along the edges on the *right side* of your canvas. The cord should lie toward the center, with its seam allowance matching the outside edge of the canvas seam allowance. Start and end in the middle of one side (preferably the bottom, as least conspicuous). The cording is now ready to be stitched onto the pillow packing along with the needlepoint front.

SEWING THE PILLOW TOGETHER

Cut the backing the same size as the pillow front, including seam allowances on all sides. Baste the backing over the needlepointed canvas on the stitching line, right sides together. If you want a zipper, insert it along one of the sides (following directions on the package) before stitching the rest of the cover. Then, *with the zipper open,* machine stitch all around the outer edges, through the three layers of canvas, cording and backing. Use the zipper foot, to come as close to the cording as possible. Then turn right side out, through the zipper opening. Insert the pillow form, close the zipper, and there you are.

If you're not using a zipper, stitch only three sides together, leaving one side open. Turn right side out, insert the pillow form, then blind-stitch the fourth side together by hand.

When the pillow cover gets dirty, unzip it and send it to be dry cleaned; or, if hand sewn, snip open the fourth side and when the cover is clean, resew it.

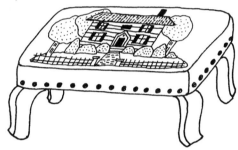

PIANO BENCH OR FOOTSTOOL COVER

If a cover already exists on the piano bench or footstool, remove it and study how it was applied. Tack the canvas along the edges with upholstery tacks, then glue some gimp upholstery braid in a complementary color over the tacks. If you prefer decorative nail heads instead of tacks and braid, use rustproof nail heads and hammer them in at ½″ (12 mm.) intervals.

TRAY OR TABLE

To use your needlepoint picture in one of these decorative but functional ways, follow the general directions in this chapter for framing. The frame should be a simple and sturdy one made of wood, and stained or painted in the color of your choice.

After the needlepoint is inserted, the frame should be backed with ¼″ plywood. This should be glued and firmly nailed all around the underside of the frame. Stain or paint the visible plywood sides to match the rest of the frame.

If making a tray, buy wrought-iron, brass or chrome cabinet handles and secure them to the sides of the frame with screws. If making a table, glue the tray to some expandable tray-table legs.

You can also set your needlepoint picture under the glass top of a coffee table or writing desk. Fold back the unworked canvas border around the needlepoint and glue to the wrong side of the canvas with white resin glue. Let dry thoroughly. Center portrait carefully on desk or table and hold in place with double-stick tape before laying the glass on top.

TOTE BAG

Your needlepoint portrait should be fairly small if you intend to use it this way. Buy an inexpensive tote bag in a solid, quiet color; the bag should have flat or slightly rounded sides. Apply white resin glue sparingly to the back of your needlepoint and glue it to the side of the bag. Then glue gimp upholstery braid in the desired color over the raw canvas edges surrounding the portrait, remembering to miter the corners of the braid.

Index

III. HOREB

Pillars - Horiz. Cobbie - frame

Stairs - long-armed CROSS/CONTINENTAL

Front Door - Mosaic, Reverse fern evezit, contin onle one row
Two.